"I have spent some hours readin[g]
to read it, and then decided to [...]
necessary for me to grasp all that Pastor Brent Rudoski had presented.

This book is written by a man who sincerely loves the church, and for a people who say they do as well. It is designed to help the bride of Christ become spotless and blameless. It's a good read, and has the feel of sitting down over a cup of coffee and having a heart-felt conversation with a man passionate in his beliefs.

I recommend you read this book. As a leader, I needed to read it; as a follower, I needed to absorb it; as a Christian, I needed to understand it; as an observer, I needed to feel like there is yet hope for positive relationship.

Read it and pass it on!"

Glen R. Stead,
Senior Pastor, Embassy Church, Prince Albert, SK
Past President, Canadian Fellowship of Churches & Ministers

"I think this is an extremely timely book that confronts the spirit of rebellion that is erupting in churches all over North America. Brent is not only exposing the ugliness and unrighteous foundations of rebellion, but he is also undermining some of the foolish assumptions of those within the "hyper-grace" movement. He speaks as a man who has personal understanding of what the stakes really are and why we should listen to his biblical insight and wisdom.

This is truly an outstanding book on discipleship and Christian maturity. Brent does a great job engaging Scripture, sharing personal stories, and helping the reader understand the practical realities of one's choices. I heartily endorse this book!"

J.D. King,
International Director of World Revival Network,
Kansas City, Missouri

"The first thing I realized as I read my good friend Pastor Brent Rudoski's new book is that Jesus was not a rebel, but the problem of rebellion lies within us.

Brent weaves this theme throughout the book, teaching that a lot of rebellion stems from the disappointments of life. He not only shows the problem, but gives us the answer.

In a world where we have excuses for everything, I thank Pastor Brent for a book of truth. Great book!"

Francis Armstrong,
Senior Pastor, Third Day Worship Centre,
Kingston, Ontario

"Some time ago, I had the privilege of spending some extended time with Pastor Brent. We were travelling together to an event, and as we drove, Brent got caught up in talking about the premise of this book. I have to admit I was not much help, as I was pretty overwhelmed at the things he was saying. We actually drove about two hours out of the way, and the only thing that stopped us was that we ended up at the Canadian/USA border.

As I read *Jesus Was Not a Rebel*, I found myself continually challenged and encouraged by the prophetic unction taken on in this book. Brent is not only a pastor, but he is a father. As a spiritual father, he is calling us to stop being moved by the rebellion that has so easily entangled us, and instead be led by another Kingdom. To quote Pastor Brent, "A real leader doesn't rise up in rebellion; he lowers himself in intercession." My hope for you is that as you read this book, you too will become overwhelmed, and you will get lost in the journey that Pastor Brent is trying to take you on."

Dustin Smith,
Integrity Worship Leader & Song Writer

"This is a good book for all believers. It reveals some issues almost every church experiences. Too many Christians are operating in rebellion and don't even know it. Pastor Brent exposes this in a very practical way. One excellent point that stood out to me in this book that God exposed in my life years ago, is that it is not about me, but about Jesus. If our attitude about church attendance is, "What is in it for me?" or "What can I get out of this church?" we are open to walking in rebellion. Instead, we ought to say, "What can I give to this church?" and "How can I serve Christ's body?" Jesus came with this attitude, and He is our Great Example. Pastor Brent challenges us on this, and expects us to respond with maturity and love."

Kim Weiler,
President & Founder of Fe Viva World Missions

"In the movie, *Back to the Future*, the lead character is constantly goaded into foolish and dangerous activities to prove he is not "chicken." Today, many believers have taken a similar line as they seek to prove that they are not "man-pleasers." As such, they are easily manipulated into lawless rebellion in order to prove that they are free moral agents. In their wake, submission has now become synonymous with oppression, as what previously was the domain of insecure teenagers has become daily manna to many. Perhaps this is a reflection of where some are as "spiritual teenagers." While this is to be preferred above remaining "spiritual children," it is not to be confused with maturity. Brent's work has isolated some great biblical guidelines pertaining to both submission and rebellion. For those who wish to press on to maturity, it will be refreshing and illuminating."

Marc Brisebois,
Senior Pastor, Spruce Grove Community Church,
Spruce Grove, Alberta

JESUS
WAS NOT
A
REBEL

JESUS WAS NOT A REBEL

BRENT RUDOSKI

JESUS WAS NOT A REBEL
Copyright © 2014 by Brent Rudoski

Unless otherwise noted, all Scripture quotations are taken from the Holman Christian Standard Bible®, Copyright © 1999, 2000, 2002, 2003, 2009 by Holman Bible Publishers. Used by permission. Scripture quotations marked (NKJV) are taken from the New King James Version®. Copyright © 1982 by Thomas Nelson, Inc. Used by permission. All rights reserved. Scripture quotations marked (NLT) are taken from the Holy Bible, New Living Translation, copyright ©1996, 2004, 2007 by Tyndale House Foundation. Used by permission of Tyndale House Publishers, Inc., Carol Stream, Illinois 60188. All rights reserved. Scripture quotations marked (ESV) are taken from The Holy Bible, English Standard Version® (ESV®), copyright © 2001 by Crossway, a publishing ministry of Good News Publishers. Used by permission. All rights reserved. Scripture quotations marked (AMP) are taken from the Amplified® Bible, Copyright © 1954, 1958, 1962, 1964, 1965, 1987 by The Lockman Foundation. Used by permission. Scripture quotations marked (MSG) are taken from The Message. Copyright © by Eugene H. Peterson 1993, 1994, 1995, 1996, 2000, 2001, 2002. Used by permission of NavPress Publishing Group. Scripture quotations marked (GW) are taken from GOD'S WORD®, © 1995 God's Word to the Nations. Used by permission of Baker Publishing Group. Scripture quotations marked (KJV) are taken from the King James Version of the Bible. Scripture quotations marked (BBE) are taken from the Bible in Basic English.

Printed In Canada

ISBN: 978-1-4866-0430-2

Word Alive Press
131 Cordite Road, Winnipeg, MB R3W 1S1
www.wordalivepress.ca

MIX
Paper from responsible sources
FSC® C016245

Cataloguing in Publication may be obtained through Library and Archives Canada

DEDICATION

I dedicate this book to the leadership of the body of Christ, in appreciation for all the blood, sweat, and tears given in service to the saints. "For God is not unjust; He will not forget your work and the love you showed for His name when you served the saints—and you continue to serve them" (Hebrews 6:10).

I also dedicate this book to the faithful people of God who have paid the price to stay connected to the church, even though it is far from perfect. "So we must not get tired of doing good, for we will reap at the proper time if we don't give up. Therefore, as we have opportunity, we must work for the good of all, especially for those who belong to the household of faith" (Galatians 6: 9–10).

This book is for all of you. You are my heroes!

CONTENTS

Acknowledgements

Pastor Ivan & Marcia Antoniuk: Without you, I would never have become the person I am today. Thank you for pioneering Faith Alive so the rest of us could follow. We are proud to carry out the vision God birthed in your hearts so many years ago. Thanks for establishing the message of faith, healing, and deliverance. I will be forever thankful.

Steve and Kathy Gray and World Revival Church: You are my good friends in revival. Thanks a million for all you have done for us. We are eternally grateful for the Spirit of God who has linked us for revival. You have taught, and we have caught so much from all of you. We will never be the same!

Thanks to all my Canadian pastor friends who have linked shields and fought side by side to see revival consume this land. You are an inspiration to me.

Faith Alive Family Church: You are amazing! Thank you for being the human guinea pigs that I had the privilege to practice these messages on. Over the years, you have been very gracious as you've allowed me to minister and speak into your lives, though not always so perfectly. You are the best!

My wonderful wife, Barbara: Thanks for always understanding. Thank you for the support you have shown over and over again. I could not do this without you. Thanks for making it easy to be in the ministry.

My son, Brinn, and his wife, Sheri, and my daughters, Bailey and Briona: You guys are awesome! You have always let us do so much in the ministry for the Lord without a complaint of any kind. I know God has and will continue to reward you for it.

Val Keen: Thank you for your help in editing. The long hours you invested are greatly appreciated. I couldn't have done it without you.

Thank you to Rebeka Wilson for the amazing cover design.

Thanks to Adam, Lorna, Jean, Kelly, and Beckie (hope I didn't forget anyone), who proofread and helped make this book the best it could be.

Last, and certainly not least, I want to honour our Lord Jesus Christ. Thank You for such a great salvation! I am in awe of who You are and what You do in all of our lives. Thank You for being God!

FOREWORD

I was delighted when Brent told me he had written a book. I was even more delighted when he asked me to write the foreword. As a pastor, author, musician, Emmy award winner, and filmmaker, I am well aware that we live in a hurting society looking for answers. I am confident that Brent, my friend for over fourteen years, has observed the ebb and flow of religion with a watchful eye and is qualified to diagnose the cause of the many spiritual, emotional, and physical ailments that have invaded our churches.

This book, Jesus Was Not a Rebel, will narrow your search for answers by helping you discover the root of rebellion that is driving so many people into foolishness and heartache.

Brent will unveil his own roots of rebellion, the results of that rebellion, and how he found his way out of it. Within these pages you will find how rebellion, though common among the religious today, is contrary to historical Christianity and the written Word of God. The book will help you see that the fruit of Jesus' ministry was based on obedience to His father and the beauty of you following His example.

Do yourself a favour and read this book carefully so that you may escape the traps of the devil made to look delicious in a hungry world searching for truth. Brent wrote this book to save you from following the deception of the rebellious that teach, as 2 Corinthians puts it, "another Jesus, another spirit and another gospel."

As a pastor and leader to the body of Christ worldwide, I can whole-heartedly endorse this book. Its teaching is significant and necessary for those who want to attain to the stature of the mature amidst the childish rebellion that is found in most churches.

Steve Gray
Senior Pastor, World Revival Church of Kansas City, Missouri

1.

WHAT'S THE
BIG DEAL?

We live in a rebellious world! The effects of this rebellion can be seen and felt in almost every person, home, and country across the globe. Ever since the fall of Adam and Eve, mankind has fought a battle between staying "inside the lines" if he wants to do right, and stepping "outside the lines" if he doesn't. This is the eternal conflict raging inside every person born into this world. The sin nature of man constantly fuels the desire to step outside of these imaginary lines and do evil. Mankind is inherently rebellious and the cause for every evil and destructive action in the world. We can only blame ourselves for the problems our rebellion has caused. The war within rages on!

If we asked the average person what they thought the world's greatest problems were, I'm sure we'd hear answers like: poverty, euthanasia, abortion, addiction, pornography, sex slavery, murder, adultery, and so on. While we can all agree about the devastation these actions have created, we must ask if there is something deeper involved within each one of these issues. The prophet Isaiah declares, "*The earth staggers like a drunkard and sways like a hut. Earth's rebellion weighs it down, and it falls, never to rise again*" (Isaiah 24:20).

Rebellion is a weight that God never intended for the earth or its inhabitants to carry. Its effects are devastating. In the book of Romans, Paul describes the consequences of rebellion as taking their toll on creation to the extent that it is now groaning, struggling to be free from the burden of rebellion thrust upon it. The earth will one day be set free from rebellion's influence when Jesus returns to restore His kingdom in its fullness.

REBELLION'S ROOTS

Is there a root cause of the evils seen in the world today, or are they an entity to themselves? Paul states, *"For just as through one man's disobedience the many were made sinners, so also through the one man's obedience the many will be made righteous"* (Romans 5:19).

Rebellion has been growing and operating since the beginning, so it's no wonder it has such a stronghold in people today. All of our struggles with authority, establishment, leadership, or stubbornness have their roots in the rebellion first manifested through Adam and Eve in the garden. Since that time, it has been allowed to take root in the hearts of men and women to their own destruction.

> *The Lord God took the man and placed him in the garden of Eden to work it and watch over it. And the Lord God commanded the man, "You are free to eat from any tree of the garden, but you must not eat from the tree of the knowledge of good and evil, for on the day you eat from it, you will certainly die."* GENESIS 2:15–17

Through one man's disobedience (rebellion against the Word of God), sin has passed down throughout history from one generation to another. Adam, the first man, who was created perfect, beautiful, sinless, and good, chose to disobey the command of His Father and Creator. All God said was, *"Do not eat from the tree of the knowledge of good and evil!"* That's it, just one command! How hard could that be? Because of that one seemingly tiny act of defiance, all mankind was infected with rebellion!

Some might say, "Perhaps he did it ignorantly, not knowing what was up." Look at what 1 Timothy 2:14 says, *"And Adam was not deceived, but the woman was deceived and transgressed."* This Scripture is clear. While Eve apparently was deceived, Adam was not. Eve transgressed— possibly believing what she did was the right decision. Remember, the person who is deceived doesn't know it—that's why it's called deception. Adam, on the other hand, was not deceived; he knew exactly what he was doing. He was violating the one and only command God had given. Adam's sin was an act of rebellion against God, so I would say the original sin was rebellion, not pride! Pride is one of the many sins resulting from rebellion, but it was not the original sin.

So many of us want to believe the original sin was pride, which we link back to Lucifer, the once glorious angel who had walked with God. While pride is a sin that also has dire consequences in the lives of mankind, it is just an off-shoot of the original sin of rebellion.

WE CAN'T IGNORE ANY TYPE OF REBELLION IN OUR LIVES, NOR TREAT IT CASUALLY.

What started out as a seed has taken root in the hearts and minds of man, and grown up into a fully mature, fruit bearing tree. That seed, which began with words telling Adam and Eve to disobey the commandments of God, has been passed down from generation to generation until the present day. We can't ignore any type of rebellion in our lives, nor can we treat it casually. Rebellion is wrong! It is not of God. It is a generational curse that God has forgiven, and He wants us delivered from its effects.

The error Adam and Eve made was in their failure to understand the outcome that would result from eating of the tree. God gave them explicit instructions not to eat of that one tree, and He told them that if they disobeyed, they would surely die. God's instructions are always for our good. Even though they may be restrictive, and irritate us sometimes, they are always for our benefit. He gave us rules to follow to protect us from what we don't know or fully understand. In this manner, His ways are certainly higher than ours! We don't have to understand the reasons for God's instructions; we just need to obey them. How many children have asked, "Why?" when their parents told them to do something? I'm sure we all remember how annoyed we were when our parents said, "Because I said so!" But the truth is we didn't need to know. Just as a parent isn't required to explain his/her every action, neither is our heavenly Father. The issue isn't whether or not we understand; the issue is our obedience. If we disobey, we become rebellious!

DEFINITION OF REBELLION

The website, www.dictionary.com, defines rebellion as, "open, organized, and armed resistance to one's government or ruler, and resistance to or defiance of any authority, control or tradition."[1] *Webster's Dictionary* defines rebellion as "open resistance to or defiance of lawful authority."[2] Rebellion occurs when a person fully understands that he is violating lawful authority, but does it anyway. In Adam's case, he disobeyed the direct Word of God, spoken from God's very mouth. Adam knew full well what he was about to do, but instead of exercising a little wisdom and restraint, he decided to rebel anyway. I can't imagine why Adam would choose to disregard the command of God, but the fact remains that he did!

Since that fateful day so long ago, the nature of rebellion has worked insidiously among men, and to this day is the root of every sin committed on the earth. Let's consider some scenarios:

- *The young child who continually refuses to heed his mother's warnings.*

- *The teenager who doesn't want to obey his parents' household rules.*

- *Adults who struggle to obey local authorities, doing so only for fear of being caught and punished.*

- *Groups who never seem to like the current government and spend considerable money, time, and labour in an effort to up-root it.*

- *People who struggle with leadership (employer, pastor, spouse, coach, teacher, and so on) and don't want to yield to anyone.*

- *The very essence of rebellion lies in its provocative temptation to disobey authority.*

The very essence of rebellion lies in its provocative temptation to disobey authority. Rebellion ensues when we decide not to follow the rules, laws, ordinances, commands, suggestions, and down to earth, godly or parental wisdom laid out before us. For example, when a parent says to their child, "Don't smoke or use drugs," they are saying it for the child's protection. The Surgeon General gives a clear warning on every package of cigarettes by saying "Smoking can kill you." Many still disregard this sound advice and start smoking anyway. The laws and rules set down are usually for our safety and protection, yet there is in us the propensity to rebel.

Let's face it—in the heart of man, there is a root of rebellion that never wants to go away. It's always lurking in the darker recesses, seeking to find a voice and an arm through which to work its evil. Man is inherently rebellious! Jeremiah 17:9 (KJV) tells us that "*The heart is ... desperately wicked; who can know* [understand] *it?*"

You may be asking, "What's the big deal? So what if a child balks at the commands of his mother? Who cares if a teenager skips school to have a little fun? Does it really matter if we disobey the government and the authorities all around us? Why can't we just do our own thing?"

Let me illustrate by talking about a movie I recently viewed called, *The Book of Eli*.[3] After a world-wide holocaust decimates the earth, a group sends a man out to collect and bring back the greatest books ever written so their value can be ascertained and utilized. The man, portrayed by actor Denzel Washington, has memorized the book that everyone seems to want. It turns out to be the Bible. As he travels, he ends up in a populated area, tightly controlled by a well-armed dictator and his band of thugs. The dictator wants this book very, very badly, and is willing to sacrifice anyone who stands in his way. Although he clearly is not a believer in God, he knows this book has the power to curb the rebellious nature of man, and create order out of almost certain chaos and upcoming anarchy. What's the point here? Without godly boundaries, set rules and laws, the world would be in anarchy with an "every man for himself" mentality.

STAY ON THE TRACKS

Rules make it easy for us to stay out of trouble. They are like the tracks on which trains travel. Stay on them and all is well; go off and ... you get the picture. In life it is the same—all things being equal, of course. If we do what is right, life will be good. If not, it could go badly for us. The people sitting in our prisons are all there for the same reason—rebellion. They chose to partake in an action that was in direct opposition to the laws established by the government placed over them by God. They chose to do wrong and are reaping the consequences. They were not forced to do it; it was their choice. We all have a choice whether or not to yield to and obey the rules.

> Everyone must submit to the governing authorities, for there is no authority except from God, and those that exist are instituted by God. So then, the one who resists the authority is opposing God's command, and those who oppose it will bring judgment on themselves. For rulers are not a terror to good conduct, but to bad. Do you want to be unafraid of the authority? Do what is good, and you will have its approval. For government is God's servant for your good. But if you do wrong, be afraid, because it does not carry the sword for no reason. For government is God's servant, an avenger that brings wrath on the one who does wrong. Therefore, you must submit, not only because of wrath, but also because of your conscience. And for this reason you pay taxes, since the authorities are God's public servants, continually attending to these tasks. –ROMANS 13:1–6

Rules and regulations are God's servants for security and continuity in society. What would society be like without proper authority, government or policing? I think we all know the answer to that one. While we may not all agree on every law or rule, we can agree that without them, society would become lawless, and absolute chaos would erupt.

RULES ARE FOR OUR PROTECTION...

What am I getting at? God doesn't want any of His people in prisons of any kind, hence the implementation of governments and laws. Rules are for our protection, both in the natural and the spiritual. If we break those laws, the consequences can be dire. Anyone who has children will understand what I'm saying. We give our children rules to follow for their own good and protection. Why? Because children are sometimes blind to the consequences of their actions. Parents are there to help them see what they cannot. For example, you tell your children not to run out onto the streets because it's dangerous. Small children don't always understand just what a four thousand pound car can do when it strikes a person. They are blind to this reality, but we are not. We give them this rule for their protection, not as a restriction on their freedoms. If they follow the rule, they may have a longer life. Many children have been struck by a vehicle when chasing a ball onto the road. The pain and anguish this caused could have been avoided if the rules were followed. Adults are not exempt from following the rules; they apply to us, as well.

This is true concerning the laws of a city, but also true in a spiritual sense. In my life, I was always prone to rebel against any rule, whether parental, godly or governmental. I never wanted to obey. I always resisted what my parents or teachers required of me. As I grew into my teens, I frequently found myself in trouble because of disobedience to some person or law. The older I got, the worse it became. Although I believed I was getting away with something by disobeying the laws or rules, in reality I was really hurting myself. Rebellion comes with a price, as every incarcerated person can attest.

> WHILE IT PROMISES FREEDOM, REBELLION ACTUALLY
> PRODUCES A LOAD NO ONE SHOULD CARRY.

Yes, rebellion demands a hefty price from any who indulge in it. While it promises freedom, rebellion actually produces a load no one should carry. When I was thirteen years old, I started a ten-year stretch of rebellion. I began to abuse alcohol and drugs, and the more I indulged, the more it cost me as I lost the ability to govern my own life. As the sin of rebellion grew in my life, the weight of it dragged me further and further down. Rebellion cost me money, relationships, self respect, and the respect of others. While I thought I was growing up, I was, in fact, growing down. By the time I turned twenty-three, my life was a total mess. I had no ambition, no education, no money, and barely a job. My drinking and smoking used up every pay cheque, all at the expense of my girlfriend and my child. My rebellion had deceived, corrupted, and taken its toll on me. I certainly needed a Saviour.

I LEARNED THAT REAL FREEDOM DOESN'T
COME FROM TRANSGRESSING THE RULES; IT COMES
FROM THE EXACT OPPOSITE—OBEYING THEM.

Finally, I gave my life to Jesus Christ. When I did, that weighty load of sin and rebellion lifted off my shoulders, and I was free. I was really free! The funny thing was I didn't realize I was bent over with that weight until it was gone. That's what rebellion does to us; it weighs us down with burdens we were never meant to carry. I learned that real freedom doesn't come from transgressing the rules; it comes from the exact opposite—obeying them. Skipping school, smoking, drinking, and taking drugs, were all doing their part to set me free from established authority. My parents used to say, "Brent, don't you start smoking; it will kill you." I remember the first cigarette I smoked. After careful planning, I stole one from my mom, waited for the cover of darkness, and crept to the park across the street. My heart was pounding and my hands were shaking as I lit up for the very first time. After coughing, sputtering, and hacking all the way through it, I convinced myself I was better for it. But was I? Where is that freedom when you try to quit years later, but fail? Isn't it that way with every rebellious idea? It promises freedom but only delivers bondage. I spent my earlier years with the belief that by stepping out of line, I could find authentic freedom. Only when I got back in line did I begin to experience the real thing.

SUSPICION AND FEAR—THE FERTILIZER OF REBELLION

Now the serpent was the most cunning of all the wild animals that the Lord God had made. He said to the woman, "Did God really say, 'You can't eat from any tree in the garden.'?" –GENESIS 3:1

Every form of rebellion begins with questions such as, *Is it actually to our benefit to listen and obey? Perhaps they made these rules for their advantage,* not ours. How dare they restrict us or try to control us! After all, Jesus died so we could be free, right? These thoughts sound so tasty, but don't you dare take a bite!

The root of rebellion has its origins in a lack of trust. The serpent did not cause rebellion; he just insinuated God really wasn't looking after their best interests. He planted the seed of rebellion with a simple thought—God was holding out on them. It is at this intersection where faith and doubt collide. Rebellion spreads easily when it works together with suspicion, mistrust, and fear.

This method has worked wonders for the enemy all these years. For rebellion to take root, all that is needed is for the seed to be planted into the mind. Adam and Eve chose to listen to the advice of the serpent instead of continuing to trust and obey the Word of God. It is the same for all of us today.

All rebellion starts the same way, and if not checked in time, it will rise up and cause trouble. Some believe that by listening to the authority figures in their lives, they are somehow being led astray, threatened, or restricted. They have believed the lie! God ordained authority for our good, to bless us and not hurt us. Do you believe that?

This root of rebellion has been passed down for generations and has its claws firmly entrenched in our fears. No one seems to be totally immune to rebellion's operations. It can still affect us today if we fail to pull it out by the roots.

*The woman said to the serpent, "We may eat the fruit from the trees in the garden. But about the fruit of the tree in the middle of the garden, God said, 'You must not eat it or touch it, or you will die.'" "No! You will not die," the serpent said to the woman. "In fact, God knows that when you eat it your eyes will be opened and you will be like God, knowing good and evil." Then the woman saw that the tree was good for food and delightful to look at, and that it was desirable for obtaining wisdom. So she took some of its fruit and ate it; she also gave some to her husband, who was with her, and he ate it. –*GENESIS 3:2–6

How did the seed of rebellion grow into such a powerful root? Suspicion was the cause, wasn't it? All the enemy had to do was plant suspicion in their minds. Eve quoted God's rules of the garden to the serpent. She knew what God said. As is often the case, the problem doesn't lie in what we know or have heard, but in whether or not we believe it. There seems to be, in all of us, a seed waiting to take hold, having its roots in suspicion, mistrust, and fear. For the most part, the seed lies dormant, but all it needs to grow is a little coaxing from a thought or voice speaking the very same ideas told to Eve. Suspicion, mistrust, and fear are the fertilizers that give power to the seed and increase its growth.

Our thinking can go like this: *Is it true? Are these rules right for me? Is this really the way it should be? Why should I listen to anyone else? Maybe I'm better off doing things my way.*

It only takes a few words or thoughts to cause a seed to germinate in our hearts. In a world where rebellion is the attitude of the day, it's no wonder churches have become affected by it. Believers can talk a good talk, but their walk doesn't always line up. All of us have been touched by rebellion at some point in our lives; it is common, familiar, and so easy to walk in. Everywhere we go we are surrounded either by rebellion itself, or by the effects of it. It is so prevalent that someone who lives an obedient, submitted, and non-rebellious life will appear odd, strange or even weird. I believe we can unknowingly operate in rebellion, as it has become so strong and powerful. It is no longer a tiny seed first spoken by Lucifer, but has matured into a full blown, fruit bearing tree. We must pull all rebellion up by the roots in our own hearts and minds. If we do, we can start putting an end to the insidious power of rebellion and its destructive forces.

THE EFFECTS OF REBELLION

We are familiar with generational curses that affect our health and contribute to heart disease, diabetes or cancer, but do you know that the sin of rebellion can also be passed down? Not only does it change hands from one family to the next, but the consequences are also passed down. This is the fruit of rebellion. Man's entire sin nature has its roots in rebellion. Sometimes we want to just zero in on a specific fault, shortcoming or sin, but what we need to focus on is rebellion. If we can get people free of rebellion, we can get them free from anything. Drug addiction, alcohol abuse, sexual problems, lying, anger, and fears of all kinds can all be defeated if their root of rebellion is pulled out.

... SOME WANTED TO BE FREE FROM THE EFFECTS OF
THEIR REBELLION, BUT NOT FROM REBELLION ITSELF.

In our church, we've prayed for many people over the years who were instantly delivered from every sin you could think of and even some you can't. God has moved supernaturally to help these people, and many have remained clean; however, some have not. I had often wondered why some could stay free and some couldn't. Was God a respecter of persons? Does this only work for some people? No, what I discovered is that some wanted to be free from the effects of their rebellion, but not from rebellion itself.

THE ROOT OF ALL SIN IS REBELLION

If we get rid of rebellion, our sin will automatically go; however, sin can linger if rebellion is allowed to stay planted in the soil of our hearts. The Israelites are a great example of this, because they continued to be slaves of their rebellion long after their deliverance from Egypt. When I read about these people, I think to myself, *How could they have been so stupid? Can't they see what's going on? How could they be in the glorious presence of God and still be so rebellious?* We, too, have brought Egypt into Israel, so to speak, and we wonder why there is so much rebellion in our churches. Perhaps it is time to do a thorough evaluation!

I'm writing this book because I want everyone to know that in order to fully experience the good life, all rebellion must be uprooted from our lives. As we come to realize that God gave us rules to follow for our good and not for evil, we can stop "fighting city hall," and instead follow the rules. I fought the law, but the law won!

It's disheartening to see people rebel against established authorities, because not only does it hurt the one rebelling, but everyone else feels the consequences as well.

I want to challenge the concept that Jesus was a rebel. Many people believe Jesus rebelled; therefore, their own rebellion is justified. They think they are identifying with Jesus, but they are deceiving themselves. My goal is to change the mindset of church-goers around the world who have become rebels. There are believers who say they love Jesus, but continually struggle to follow God's laws and adhere to His established authority. This rebellion reveals that they have been deceived. Jesus made the importance of this very clear in the Gospel of John when He said, *"If you love me, you will keep my commands"* (John 14:15). For those who genuinely do love Jesus, the very idea of rebelling against His Word is distasteful!

> *We all went astray like sheep; we all have turned to our own way; and the Lord has punished Him for the iniquity of us all.*
>
> —ISAIAH 53:6

> *Therefore I will give Him the many as a portion, and He will receive the mighty as spoil, because He submitted Himself to death, and was counted among the rebels; yet He bore the sin of many and interceded for the rebels.* —ISAIAH 53:12

As you read these verses, you can see Jesus went to the cross to bear the sins of all mankind. Yes, He was counted as a rebel, but He never rebelled. He took the rebellion (sin) of mankind on Himself so we could be free from its grasp and influence in our lives today.

IF HE WAS REBELLIOUS, THERE'S NO WAY
HE COULD HAVE TAKEN OUR REBELLION.
THAT WOULD BE A CONTRADICTION!

Everything Jesus did on the cross was substitutionary in nature. He was pierced for our transgressions, bruised so we could be healed, and His obedience, even unto death, was to pay for our rebellion. He bore our sin; therefore, sin has lost its power. Because He became diseased and sick on the cross, we can be healed. In addition, since He carried our rebellious nature on Himself to His death, we no longer need to rebel in life. If He was rebellious, there's no way He could have taken our rebellion. That would be a contradiction!

God has not called us to rebel, but to obey His every Word. He gave us a wonderful example to follow: His Son, Jesus, was obedient to all the laws, both natural and spiritual. Jesus paid a terrible price to save us from our rebellious nature. So you see, rebellion is a huge deal and shouldn't be taken lightly.

By the time you have read the last page of this book, I pray you will have gained some understanding of what I am trying to say. My hope is for you to realize that any and all rebellion has nothing to do with Jesus. Being rebellious identifies us with Satan and not with our Saviour and Lord, Jesus Christ. Jesus was not, never has been, and never will be a rebel!

2.

Hiding in
PLAIN SIGHT

I think we need to re-evaluate our concept of what rebellion looks like. If we picture it in the form of a Harley riding, leather clad, anti-establishment biker with long hair and a beard, or a sign-carrying demonstrator who protests on the streets of Ottawa or Washington, then most of society would be innocent. With these obvious outward characteristics, this type is obvious for all to see; but there is another. It is characterized by a *subtle stubbornness* that goes almost unnoticed, and most people fail to recognize it. This rebellion could be living in that nice couple pushing a baby carriage down the street. It could be residing in the politicians who are currently leading and guiding our country, or it might even be in the policeman who keeps watch over our city.

Sometimes the best hiding spot is right in plain sight! It frequently clothes itself under the guise of submission, but manifests as a person who is difficult to work with and always wants to do things their way. It is revealed in the failure to listen to sound advice, take correction, or act humbly. Rebellion is far more prevalent in society than most realize or care to admit, and has within it a strong resistance to established authority. It is destructive and will bear bad fruit as time passes. Whether obvious or camouflaged, rebellion must be discerned and avoided by the believer!

For rebellion is as the sin of witchcraft, and stubbornness is as iniquity and idolatry. Because you have rejected the word of the Lord, he has also rejected thee from being king.
—1 Samuel 15:23, NKJV

In order to better understand and deal with this issue, we must put it under the magnifying glass of God's Word and see what we can find. The Word of God will be our guide in finding the truth concerning what it looks like, what it does, and how it sounds. Most people have heard a sermon or two about King Saul's unwillingness to fully obey and the consequences that followed, but we're going to look at it one more time. The fact that rebellion and stubbornness are recorded in the same verse speaks volumes. Saul rebelled by deciding to only partially obey God's instructions. He told Samuel that he had done all he told him to do, but the prophet rightly disagreed. When a person doesn't fully obey, and decides to do it his own way, God calls it rebellion by stubbornness.

Rebellion can be summed up in one word—stubbornness! As believers, we have found a unique way of disguising rebellion in our lives. When we manifest a rebellious attitude, we like to pass it off as being harmlessly stubborn or strong-willed. At www.wordnet.princeton. edu, stubbornness is defined as: "The trait of being difficult to handle or overcome; resolute adherence to your own ideas or desires."[4] James writes, "But the wisdom from above is first pure, then peace-loving, gentle, compliant, full of mercy and good fruits, without favoritism and hypocrisy" (James 3:17, emphasis added).

The book of James tells us that if a person is walking in the fruits of righteousness, he will manifest a willingness to work with others in a humble, *compliant* spirit, and be able to give in to the requests of others. A person who is delivered from stubbornness has no problem with authority. A rebellious person will struggle with allowing someone else to have even the slightest control over him.

Stubbornness is not a character trait that we should be proud of; instead, we must flee from such behaviour with all our strength. Some people are proud of their so-called freedom from others and believe it to be a godly trait, and thus exhibit it with great gusto and strength. They don't realize Jesus would never have lived in such a manner. Jesus was totally submitted to authority of every kind and was very willing to work with others. He was not rebellious nor was He stubborn to the wants or desires of others. He truly was meek and humble! He is the one we should model our lives after.

Parents experience this scenario of stubbornness all the time. They ask their child to do something. He says, "Okay," but doesn't obey. If he was truly listening, he would have fulfilled what was asked of him. Rebellion starts out innocently enough when we hear but don't fully obey. Perhaps it started when we were children. We bawled and threw fits until our parents accommodated our stubbornness. I have often encountered this scene in the local supermarket. While pushing my cart down the aisle, I see a real life act of stubbornness lived out by a child and his or her embarrassed parents. I usually watch to see whether the parents are aware or ignorant of what is transpiring before them. By allowing it to continue, the unknowing parents give strength and power to the spirit of rebellion.

Rebellion is more often revealed through stubbornness than through someone who is openly defiant. Because of this, we can easily overlook rebellion when it is disguised as stubbornness. We may not like it when someone is being obstinate, but we don't treat it as we would open rebellion. Rebellion, concealed in the form of inflexibility, obstinacy, and stubbornness, can really wreak havoc, because we tend to overlook it.

How many times have we struggled to hear and obey, or take advice when it was given? Could it be we have unknowingly allowed the stronghold of rebellion to take root in our lives because it was disguised under a different name? Perhaps there is rotten fruit growing up in our hearts and minds, but we wonder how in the world did it ever get there?

PARTIAL OBEDIENCE IS STILL DISOBEDIENCE

A father decided to run some errands and told his son to wash the dishes before he returned. The son went to the kitchen to obey, but suddenly noticed the floor was a mess. Instead of doing the dishes, he chose to wash the floor, scrubbing it until it was polished and shiny. *Wow,* he thought to himself, *my father will be very pleased with me!* When the father returned, he found his son beaming from ear to ear, believing he had been obedient and, therefore, worthy of praise. Instead, the son saw something else in the eyes of his father. It was a look of disappointment, not pride.

"What did you do? Why didn't you do the dishes?" he asked his son. The son explained that he noticed the floor was really dirty, and felt he should wash it. Disappointed, the father said, "Son, I never asked you to wash the floor; I asked you to do the dishes!"

What a person wants to do, and what he should do, is not always the same thing!

Rebellion tends to do what it thinks is right instead of doing what it was asked. It always wants to do its own thing. God isn't interested in man changing the rules or doing his own thing. He desires obedience, knowing it is the key to bringing blessings to mankind. What a person wants to do, and what he should do, is not always the same thing! *"There is a way that seems right to a man, but its end is the way to death"* (Proverbs 14:12).

Saul only partially obeyed the Word of God given to him by the prophet, Samuel. Like many others, Saul believed he had fully obeyed the Lord. In reality, he had walked in rebellion by changing what he did mid-stride. Rebellion brings curses, but full obedience produces the blessings of God. Stubbornness in our hearts will cause rebellion to gain a stronghold in our lives. Don't be deceived, even a little must be avoided! A little leaven affects the whole lump! How many times have you thought, *If only I had listened, then I wouldn't have gotten into this mess?*

I have seen this played out many times in the church world. People come in to receive counsel, hear it, and then do the exact opposite of what they were instructed to do. In fact, I have spoken the Word of God to many people who immediately told me they don't believe it, or they just can't live it out. For some, it's easier to go by what they think, feel or believe, than to obey God's Word.

John 8:32, which states, *"You will know the truth and the truth will set you free,"* is often used improperly. Until it is acted upon, truth, or knowledge, will not set you free. This is why many people are still bound by the evils of their past. If a person truly wants to be free, there is nothing that can stop them. Our greatest enemy is not the devil, our past, or our wounds. The most persistent enemy of our freedom is our rebellion! When we cling to the past, we can never go forward. We will always struggle to be happy when we blame our unhappiness on past hurts. If we stubbornly hang on to our own thinking, we will never be free. We must let go of it and renew our minds to God's way of being and doing.

Many who struggle to find freedom from certain sins, habits or addictions, may not be dealing with the right issue. Sometimes the root of their problem is rebellion. Often, those habitual patterns are the outward manifestation of a stubborn heart. Rebellion is a powerful root with the strength to empower evil. I've dealt with many people over the years that seemed to be bound by one thing or another. I mistakenly believed the root cause was the addiction itself, but it often turned out to be old-fashioned rebellion. The stubborn determination to cling to their own way of thinking or doing kept them bound up.

Rebellion isn't difficult to figure out. It is simply this: I want to do it MY way! Now, I am not saying we don't have hurts or pains to deal with, but often when people struggle to be free, it is because they don't want to do it God's way. They may not even understand this insidious root called rebellion, but it is there nonetheless.

We don't necessarily see our own rebellion, because it is hidden within the framework of our own thinking. Instead of labeling it as rebellion, we call it, "doing it my way," or "this is what I want to do," or "this is how I see it." Rebellion is easily concealed, because most of us don't believe our thoughts or ways of doing things could ever be wrong.

"GOD TOLD ME"

How many times has the phrase, "God told me," been used to justify a person's unscriptural actions? I remember one guy who insisted God had told him not to work, but to "live by faith." The Bible says if a man doesn't work, he shouldn't eat. A friend of mine once had no less than five women claiming him as their future husband. They simultaneously believed they heard the voice of God. Then there's the person who decides to divorce his or her spouse to marry another, because "God said!" I could go on and on, but you get the picture. It's easy to be misled by one's own thoughts and pass them off to be the voice of the Lord.

People pull the "God told me," card out of the deck whenever they disagree with counsel, are offended, or decide to leave the church. It amazes me how that card never comes out until they disagree or are offended! Why is it that God always seems to *speak* so clearly about leaving a church *after* a person is hurt or offended? Does God only talk when a person is hurt, or is it plain, old fashioned rebellion hiding behind those famous words? Who can disagree with someone who says, "God told me?" If God actually spoke to them, who are we to contradict Him? Can you see how easy it is for rebellion to hide? Rebellion flaunts itself under the very name of God and hides best in plain sight! What we need to learn is this: every thought we think isn't necessarily right or true. This is why we need the Word of God and the wise counsel of others in our lives.

Leave the Past Behind

> You can get the people out of Egypt,
> but can you get Egypt out of the people?

How many times did God call His chosen people rebellious? They followed Him into of slavery and into freedom, only to find they were still slaves to rebellion long after they left Egypt. It's funny how they despised the rebellious nation they had been enslaved to, yet struggled to overcome rebellion within themselves. It's so easy for us to hate the rebellion in others, but never even notice it within ourselves. You can get the people out of Egypt, but can you get Egypt out of the people?

> The Israelites were guilty of moving forward on
> the outside, but going backwards on the inside.

The Israelites were guilty of moving forward on the outside, but going backwards on the inside. There have been many times when a person comes into our church and is wonderfully saved and filled with the Holy Ghost. The first thing they are told is, "Don't go back to where you came from, do what you used to do, or hang with your old friends!" When they heed those instructions, there is almost a one hundred percent victory rate, but when they don't, failure is inevitable. Many times Jesus told the recently delivered person to follow Him, and not return to where he came from. Some were able to keep their newfound freedom, and others were not. Why? The root of rebellion was still at work. When we refuse to leave the past behind, we are clinging to our rebellious roots instead of to the Lord.

While trying to find the source of people's problems, we often look in the wrong places. We see the disguise but miss the root cause. In this case, the mask is disobedience to wise counsel while the root is rebellion. We have found that people who give up their old opinions, ideas, and reasoning to truly follow the Word of God, live in a higher form of freedom.

THE BLIND SPOT

Arrogance leads to nothing but strife, but wisdom is gained by those who take advice. —PROVERBS 13:10

Have you ever made a mistake in life because you did something that seemed right in your own eyes, but it ended up in disaster? Have you felt so sure about doing something, only to see it backfire? Is it possible that what we think is right is not always the truth, the whole truth, and nothing but the truth, so help me God?

One of the worst things we can do is believe we are infallible and right in every situation. While many of us don't believe we could ever be deceived, it is astounding how many times we have erred due to our own arrogance. Could we be arrogant and not know it? I can speak from personal experience, having made many rash decisions that cost me greatly because I did what was right in my own eyes. If I had listened to the advice that was spoken to me at the time, I would have saved myself tremendous heartache and pain.

The truth of the matter is we all have blind spots. You know what that is, don't you? It is that unseen area that our side and rear view mirrors fail to pick up. This is why our driving instructors teach us to shoulder check before we change lanes. Unless we make the effort to turn our neck and look, we'll never see what's there.

Could it be that we all have blind spots in life? I can look back to a far younger me who thought he had all the answers to life. In my arrogant youth, I made many mistakes that bore bad fruit. That rebellion and stubbornness deceived me by lying to me, telling me I had the right answers and all would be okay. Boy, was I ever blind!

When I was first saved, it was an extremely exciting time in my life. God was moving, and all things were new, but there were blind spots, obvious and glaring to others, but unknown to me. After being in the church for a while, some of the people there began saying things to me that I didn't think were true. They said self-pity and rejection were hindering my life. Of course, thinking I knew everything, I completely rejected the idea. Do you want to know what really bugs me about people who think they know everything? It gives a bad name to those of us who do—ha-ha!

One evening as I was falling asleep, the Lord spoke to me. He said, "Brent, what they are saying is true, and you need to go in and get some help." Self-pity will destroy you if you let it. It is a force that doesn't let go easily. It works well alongside rejection, and next to each other, the two are like dynamite and fire. Eventually, there is going to be an explosion. I went in, received prayer, and was set free. What's the point? I had some blind spots that were working to destroy me, and if God hadn't spoken, my life might still be a mess today. I'm so thankful God spoke to me, but why didn't I listen to the people who were telling me the same thing? I could have experienced victory long before if I had only listened.

THE DONKEY SPEAKS

Do you remember the story of Balaam? The Moabite king, Balak, sent elders with money to bribe Balaam to curse the Israelites. Balaam invited them to spend the night and said he would give them an answer in the morning. That night, God instructed Balaam not to go with them, for he was not to curse what God had blessed. The next morning, the elders returned with the news that Balaam would not come. Undaunted, Balak sent higher ranking officials to Balaam, in the hopes of changing his mind. Again, Balaam refused. I can imagine him saying something like this: "If they give me all the gold in China, I could not go against the command of the Lord, but I'll tell you what—stay the night and I'll see what else the Lord will say." That night, the Lord spoke to Balaam again and said he should go with the men, but he was only to do what God told him to do. The next morning, Balaam saddled his donkey and went with the officials of Moab.

As Balaam went, God became angry and sent an angel to bar the way. The donkey saw the angel and veered off the path, so Balaam struck her in an effort to get her back in line. Three times the same thing happened, until finally the donkey dropped to the ground. Balaam was incensed and began to beat her. Then the Lord opened the donkey's mouth, and she said, "What have I done to you that you have beaten me these three times?"

Balaam replied, "You have made me look like a fool. If I had a sword, I would kill you right now."

She spoke again, "Am I not your faithful ride even until this day? Have I ever treated you this way before?"

Balaam's obvious answer was "no." No, she hadn't (By now, wouldn't you think something very fishy was going on?). Balaam probably wondered why in the world he was having a conversation with his donkey.

It was at this time that God opened Balaam's eyes to see the angel, who informed him that had it not been for his faithful steed, he would already be dead. Yikes! Thank God the donkey could see what the great and mighty seer could not. When God has to use an animal to get our attention, maybe, just maybe, we aren't listening.

Why was God angry with Balaam? Didn't He initially tell him to go with Balak's men? What caused the sudden change? It was this— Balaam wasn't paying attention to what was going on in his own heart. Even though he denied it, Balaam secretly wanted the silver and gold he was previously offered, and God would never allow Balaam to curse the Israelites to get it. He was angry because He knew Balaam's heart was not pure, but full of greed.

Why am I telling this story? Balaam didn't listen to the instructions already given to him by God. His desire for gold and silver hindered his ability to hear and obey the truth. Have we ever done that? God gives us His Word and sends people to speak into our lives, but because of our selfish desires, we ignore those voices, so God has to use a donkey (in whatever form He chooses) to get our attention. Like Balaam, we may think we see it all clearly, but do we?

I have often wondered how many times God has sent braying donkeys to get my attention. Why didn't I listen to the people speaking into my life? Why did I have to hear from God directly? God tried to talk to me through the people in my life, but I was too stubborn to hear. He did eventually speak to me, but it was only as a last resort.

I BELIEVE THERE ARE TIMES THAT IF GOD HAS TO SPEAK TO US DIRECTLY, IT'S QUITE POSSIBLE WE ARE WALKING IN SOME FORM OF STUBBORNNESS OR REBELLION.

I believe there are times that if God has to speak to us directly, it's quite possible we are walking in some form of stubbornness or rebellion (I can hear the sputtering, so relax; I'm not saying that every time God speaks to us, we are in rebellion). God speaks to us in many ways; it is up to us to hear and obey. Just as Balaam, the mighty prophet, refused to listen to his donkey, we too can dismiss the vessels through which God chooses to speak to us. It's time to stop ignoring the people speaking the truth into our lives because we are so bent on hearing it straight from the mouth of God.

REBELLION IS THE BLIND SPOT OF LIFE

Fools think they need no advice, but the wise listen to others.
—PROVERBS 12:15, NLT

The truth was I was blinded by my own rebellion. You see, rebellion is the cause of many of our troubles. It is like the blind spot that none of us can see. Many accidents could be prevented if people would simply shoulder check instead of choosing to trust only in what they see in the mirror.

The same can be said of trusting our own ideas instead of heeding what those around us have to say. We believe our own mirrors (what we think) instead of looking to others for wisdom and guidance. God uses people as mirrors to show us our blind spots. The question is: are we willing to accept what they reveal?

EASILY MANIFESTED—NOT EASILY REMOVED

> *But be doers of the word and not hearers only, deceiving yourselves.*
> *Because if anyone is a hearer of the word and not a doer, he is like a*
> *man looking at his own face in a mirror. For he looks at himself, goes*
> *away, and immediately forgets what kind of man he was. But the*
> *one who looks intently into the perfect law of freedom and perseveres*
> *in it, and is not a forgetful hearer but one who does good works—*
> *this person will be blessed in what he does.* —JAMES 1:22–25

Many mirrors are available to help us see the best way to go, should we choose to look in them. Some of the mirrors God has provided to reflect and reveal the truth are His Word, the Holy Spirit, people, and even our own experiences. Marriage is an excellent example of a mirror. Our spouse speaks truth to us, but we fail to hear it. Then we hear the same thing from the pulpit, a famous speaker, or in some book we are reading, and suddenly, the light comes on! Remember Balaam—a donkey spoke to him. God will use whatever means are at His disposal. When we take heed to the truth, it will set us free, no matter how it is revealed.

Thank God for His Word. Thank God for people who can help us see what we cannot. Thank God for our spouses. If you have one, you know they can definitely see what you cannot. Help is available to us, but will we take heed to it? The Spirit of the Lord is continually working in our lives to reveal our blind spots to us.

MOVEMENT WITHOUT WISDOM

Anytime we act without considering the situation from every angle, we run the risk of causing further repercussions. We trust what we see in the mirror of our own making instead of taking the time and energy to thoroughly check the situation out and study our next move from every angle. We make decisions based only on what we know, instead of slowing down to ask questions and listen to the wisdom of others. As we listen and obey, the blind spots of life are eliminated, and peace and reward are the results.

So now, my sons, listen to me. Never stray from what I am about to say: Stay away from her! Don't go near the door of her house! If you do, you will lose your honor and will lose to merciless people all you have achieved. Strangers will consume your wealth, and someone else will enjoy the fruit of your labor. In the end you will groan in anguish when disease consumes your body. You will say, "How I hated discipline! If only I had not ignored all the warnings! Oh, why didn't I listen to my teachers? Why didn't I pay attention to my instructors? I have come to the brink of utter ruin, and now I must face public disgrace."

–Proverbs 5: 7–14, NLT

THE TRUTH IS THAT REBELLION OR STUBBORNNESS
WILL ALWAYS PRODUCE BAD RESULTS!

These verses are referring to a simple man lured into the arms of a woman, who was not his wife, causing disaster in his life. The first eight chapters of Proverbs exhort people to pay attention and do what is right. They speak of the ills that come when we stray from righteous knowledge and wisdom to seek out our own desires and ways. The truth is that rebellion or stubbornness will always produce bad results!

As I reminisce about my younger days, I see how stubbornness and rebellion became the catalyst for many of the troubles I had, but I still blamed someone or something else for them. I resisted the instruction of others, thinking they didn't know what was right for me. If you pushed me, I pushed back! Whenever someone wanted me to do a specific thing, I was driven to do the opposite. Amazingly enough, I even believed my stubbornness was something to be proud of. What it actually did was cause the blind spot to become bigger and bigger until it was an all-consuming force. The book of Proverbs states: *"Instruct the wise, and they will be even wiser. Teach the righteous, and they will learn even more"* (Proverbs 9:9, NLT) and, *"A reproof enters more into a wise man than an hundred stripes into a fool"* (Proverbs 17:10, KJV).

A truly wise man will receive advice and correction no matter what age he is. Wisdom doesn't necessarily come with age. I have seen both the foolish and the wise among the young and the old. It is, however, quite repulsive and disappointing to see an older person acting in a very foolish manner: *"A beautiful woman who lacks discretion is like a gold ring in a pig's snout"* (Proverbs 11:22, NLT).

Some things just don't look right. A gold ring in a pig's snout, I don't think so! A beautiful woman lacking sense is not right. How about a granny wearing clothes meant for a teenager and trying to look sexy? Ewww, not a good fit!

A gold ring isn't a right fit for a pig, nor is it seemly for a believer to stubbornly refuse to listen to wise counsel. While there may be times when a lack of maturity will cause a young person to struggle with listening and obeying, it shouldn't be seen in adults, especially among church people. I have also seen young people who yield to sound instruction, serve the Lord without reservation, and obey without hesitation. It is a joy to see! The Bible tells us they will be blessed. Rebellion is not a good fit for the believer, no matter the age!

RULES DON'T BREED REBELLION

God's Word is an instruction book given to help us know, understand, and obey His will. Without it, the world would be in a chaotic mess, leading to anarchy, and resulting in destruction and death. Some people struggle with rules of any kind, thinking they are restrictive and controlling. Just think for a moment—what kind of world would it be if there were no rules to follow? Those who think it would be great are ignorant of the truth. Without rules, there is nothing to guide our conduct. God gave us rules to follow to keep us from self-destructing!

> RULES DON'T BREED REBELLION; THEY
> JUST BRING IT TO THE SURFACE.

In the church that I pastor, we put ropes along the sides of the chairs that we don't want anyone to sit on. Our ushers repeatedly tell me about visiting Christians—yes, I said Christians—who struggle with following a simple rule. They fight, fuss, and demand their own way. Unbelievable! This unwillingness to yield causes grief for everyone around. These people think they are exercising their freedom in Christ, but in reality, they're being rebellious. Has our fear of being "under the law" negated our ability to yield to a simple request? Being yielded or submitted to a rule is not coming under the law! If, as a parent, I ask my teenage daughter to clean up her room, can she say to me, "Why do I have to listen; I'm under grace, and not law?" Do we really understand the difference between law and grace? Is it possible we have taken it too far out of context? At any rate, believers can struggle with authority, rules or laws, for fear of operating under the law and not under grace. A wise friend of mine once said, "Rules don't breed rebellion; they just bring it to the surface!"

The interesting thing is that the majority of unbelievers who come into our sanctuary seem quite content to sit wherever they are asked. For some reason, they lack that rebellious attitude when they come into the church. What's up with that? Why can't the believers be this way? Why do some believers make a fuss every time they are asked to do something, especially a thing as small and insignificant as where they are to sit? They threaten never to come back saying, "They are trying to restrict, control, and hinder us from doing whatever we want. They are so legalistic!"

This may seem like a minor issue, and it probably is, but perhaps it is indicative of a greater problem in the body of Christ. If all it takes is some minor thing to get us up in arms, is it possibly a symptom of a much greater problem?

Some may ask, "Why do you do that? Why not just let them sit wherever they want?" The main reason is that we are trying to create an atmosphere for the Lord to move freely in. We also want a corporate gathering where everyone is helping each other worship the Lord in an unhindered way. We don't want someone way in the back doing their own thing, or feeling like they are on the outside looking in. It's important for everyone to be of one heart and one mind in worship.

The problem is we are so accustomed to being rebellious that we no longer recognize it in ourselves. I grew up in a home where everyone smoked, and none of us ever really noticed it. We had become desensitized to the smell, smoke, and haze in the air. In fact, we thought it was normal life. This is what happens when we live in an environment or culture of rebellion—it becomes so familiar we stop noticing it. A person can be rebellious, or stubborn, and not even know it. It isn't until after we are apart from it that we begin to see it for what it truly is. I haven't lived at home for many years now, but when I visit, I see and feel all the effects of the smoke. It's so obvious now. It affects my breathing, hurts my eyes, irritates my lungs, and the smell lingers on my clothing long after I leave. What I once thought was normal has become abnormal and uncomfortable. The same can be said of rebellion and stubbornness.

THE BLIND LEAD THE BLIND

Imagine seeing two blind people walking together as one tries to lead the other. If the person being led knew that the one leading him was blind, do you think he would continue to follow? No, it is foolish to believe a blind person could effectively lead another blind person. Jesus said, *"Hypocrite! First take the log out of your eye, and then you will see clearly to take the speck out of your brother's eye."*(Matthew 7:5).

Makes sense, doesn't it? Yet, why does it seem so hard for us to give up our pride, our stubbornness and our rebellion to hear what someone else has to say? Are we blind to our blind spots? I think we are. We are in desperate need of someone to point out our blind spots so we can avoid life's pitfalls. "I once was blind, but now I see," isn't just a beautiful song lyric talking about our initial salvation. It can be applied to the blindness of our hearts right here and now. God has provided mirrors. Isn't it time to allow them to show you a better way? If you are willing and obedient, you will eat the good of the land. Your improved sight will produce a harvest of good fruit in your life.

3.

WHAT'S WRONG
WITH
NORMAL?

D o you remember the very first time you went ripping down the road on your brand new ten-speed bike (I know; I just dated myself)? Finally, you had the bike of your dreams, just like all your friends had. You loved that bike; it was your constant companion, helper, and friend. It served you faithfully and was always there for you. It was everything you needed at the time. You were riding along doing well, the bike operating at full capacity and efficiency, but suddenly, you lost control and wiped out. You and your bike became intimately acquainted as you skidded, tumbled, and rolled onto the road. When you finally stopped, you were covered with scrapes on your elbows and knees. It was painful, wasn't it? Your precious bike had let you down and caused you great pain. What did you do? Did you toss that two-wheel bike and opt for the funky new three-wheel version? Did you question whether the bike was for you or not? Did you wonder about the sanity of all those who were still riding bikes? Didn't they know bikes were imperfect, dangerous, and capable of letting you down? No, you got up, brushed yourself off, and like me, probably got back on that bike and slowly made your way home so mom could apply peroxide, or worse, iodine.

Even though you were hurt, you never had one thought of getting rid of your bike. What a ludicrous thought! Yet isn't that what Christians do all the time? They give up on church—the very thing that has loved, helped, encouraged, strengthened, and matured them up to this point. What started out as a great institution, an incredible place of fellowship and powerful help, is now regarded with suspicion and confusion. Never would they have done anything so drastic with their bike, so I have to ask: Why is it so easy to give up on the church?

IS THE GRASS GREENER?

Have you ever gone to a pasture and studied the bovines (cows) in their natural element? I find it fascinating to see them force their heads through the barbed wire fence, risking injury, trying to eat the grass on the other side. They may not know this, but the grass on the other side is the same as the grass on this side! The grass tastes the same on both sides of the fence. In fact, many a cow has wormed its way out of the safe zone behind the fence and ended up in the ditch or on the road, looking for better grass. Are you getting the idea?

I've observed people for many years and have come to the realization that many of them have a "grass is greener" concept of life. For some reason, they think if they change churches, jobs, careers, wives/husbands, or friends, they will find a better life. Nothing could be further from the truth! The problem is not their situation or location, but the condition of their own hearts! True happiness cannot be found by changing our circumstances; it can only be found by putting our hope and faith in Christ. He alone is our sufficiency and fulfillment.

Now before you misunderstand what I'm saying, let me make something very clear. I'm not saying we should never change jobs, careers, churches, or geographical locations. I'm only saying that our motivations for doing so need to be thoroughly examined before making such decisions.

> I know how to be brought low, and I know how to abound. In any and every circumstance, I have learned the secret of facing plenty and hunger, abundance and need. I can do all things through him who strengthens me. –PHILIPPIANS 4:12–13, ESV

It's easier to look at our own hearts and change what is there than to believe the proverbial, *If I only had,* or *if this could happen,* or *I only wish.* If we can't be happy where God has us right now, we won't be any happier if we leave church, get a new job, or change geographical locations.

EXTREME EVERYTHING

Has the church become full of pleasure seekers instead of God seekers? Is it hard for you to go to church without thinking it is monotonous or uninteresting? Does the preaching of the Word weary you? Are you more interested in the excitement of the world than in the regular things of God? Can the normal activities of God even compete with the excitement and thrills experienced at the local moving picture studio?

Have you been to a movie lately? What was it like? It is amazing how fun and exciting they are. Most movies are an adrenaline rush, awesome to look at, wonderful to the ears, and a constant emotional high from start to finish. I remember watching movies from the sixties and seventies and thought they were extremely entertaining, but when I watch them now, they seem to be slow moving, less emotional, and not nearly as exciting as I thought they were. *Jaws* and *The Exorcist* were considered two of the most captivating films of their day, but if they were watched today, most people would be bored to tears! No doubt about it, we have upped our adrenaline level! Now you say, what's the big deal? Well, I am glad you asked, because I see the consequences of it in our lives. We are becoming emotional addicts! We're so used to the extremes in life that normal is no longer acceptable or desired, hence, our continued need for greater extremes! What used to be normal and fun is no longer good enough. We have become emotional addicts, always needing just a little bit more to be satisfied.

Look at the commercials on television. You can find extreme everything: deodorant, sports, energy drinks, food, travel, lifestyles, and people. Normal just doesn't seem to cut it anymore. We even have extreme church! We have created a generation of extremists that are obsessed with being anything but normal. Many feel normal is boring, or outdated. They think boring is what their parents are. Everyday life is just too narrow of a way to live. They think the only way out is to do something outrageous or, "out of the box." If life isn't a thrill a minute, people seem to feel gypped or cheated of satisfaction, but there's a problem going unnoticed here.

The desire for the extreme is creating a people who have lost touch with reality!

At this juncture, rebellion can easily creep in. People begin to rebel against the norms of life, the daily routine, the regular job, and the like. Because of this aversion to normal, anything that smacks of it is being shunned. Normal life to them is akin to touching a leper or getting the plague; however, the reality is that most of life is lived in the norms. The desire for the extreme is creating a people who have lost touch with reality. They routinely skip over the mundane as they seek to experience the rush of the extreme, but when it's all said and done, they must return home to Normalville!

The problem with all of this is that it is affecting the church. People who are accustomed to the extremes of life expect to see it in the church, as well. So, if church is "business as usual," they become dissatisfied and disillusioned with it. I mean, how can regular church even hope to compete with the awesome rush of a high voltage moving picture? Movies were created for one thing—to move the audience. They are designed to extract the most out of the viewers. Most of our church experiences cannot compete. I think many have left the church in search of a more extreme experience as they try to satisfy the itch the world has marked them with.

Experience Junkies

If we are not aware, we can become what I call *experience junkies*. By that, I mean we are no longer gratified without having some kind of thrilling experience. It's like a drug user who, after being hooked on the high of the drug, struggles to function in daily life. Regular life is not satisfying anymore, and the experience of the drug creates the illusion of a wonderful life. It is, of course, an illusion. While giving the user the appearance of life, it ends up initiating the opposite effect. That is the danger of using drugs; they create such a stimulating hallucinogenic feeling that when one comes down from it, the craving for more is intense. Users are hooked on the feeling; their bodies become addicted, and it overrules their senses. When addiction comes, the need for the experience outweighs all common sense.

We must remember that life isn't always lived out in the radical experience times, but also on the lowly plains of normal, and sometimes, even down in the valley of disappointment and discouragement.

Because of people's growing desire for extreme experiences, it is becoming more and more challenging to find satisfied believers. Think of the effect this has on a pastor, who is continually under pressure to come across as the perfect leader. He must be the humorous, non-offensive, ever smiling, politically correct, and theologically sound minister, who caters to everyone's personal agenda. People want a technologically advanced church, complete with the latest gadgets and gizmos, including laser light shows, smoke machines, million dollar sound systems, state of the art projection screens, and theatre seats equipped with holders for popcorn and drinks. Without these amusements, it is hard to keep their attention, because they feel it's not exciting or radical enough. If you have to use camel rides to draw people, you will have to continue using camels to keep them.

Instead of being content, people exhibit an attitude of discontent within the church. They start looking for the cause of their so-called problem, and the answer they come up with is "normal" church (whatever that is for them). They begin longing for the extreme church where they can be thrilled again. Has our longing for thrills and chills replaced our excitement and passion for Jesus? This unhappiness with normal can be an entry point for rebellion.

We struggle with what is normal because of our unfulfilled desire for an experience and our dissatisfaction with what is right in front of our very eyes. I'm not against modern methods and technology, but we need to learn to enjoy what is before us, whether it is thrilling or not. Our desire for the thrill a minute church experience must never replace the basics of the Word, worship, and fellowship.

This discontentment leads people to search for an external solution to an internal conflict.

It's easy to lose our purpose and identity within the church when it becomes familiar or common to us. It seems we have a hard time living in the middle ground of life and always want to experience the extreme. Paul said, "... *godliness with contentment is great gain*" (1 Timothy 6:6). Marriage is an excellent example of this. Many couples start out with so much hope and expectation about the life they are about to embark on. They believe marriage will bring the fulfillment of all their dreams and expectations. After a while, they get to know each other and settle down into regular life, having lost their initial excitement. Their eyes wander, and they start fantasizing, *I wish... If only...* This discontentment leads people to search for an external solution to an internal conflict.

**CHURCH WAS NOT DESIGNED MERELY
FOR YOUR PLEASURE OR HAPPINESS.**

Church was not designed merely for your pleasure or happiness; God designed it for His plans, purposes, and mission on the earth. If we are ever going to see His purpose fulfilled, we have to lose that thrill-a-minute mentality and realize it is all about Him.

Don't misunderstand me; there is no one who wants to have an exciting and powerful church experience more than I do. I get it, but there are those who are using the experience of God in the same way as an addict uses drugs—for the rush it gives. That is why it is dangerous to make church all about us and how we feel. Church was originally about meeting together as believers to worship and extol our great and mighty God. It was and still is all about Him. If we make it about just the experience of Him, we run the risk of taking the whole idea of "the experience" out of context. Needless to say, as much fun as it is to have frequent mountain top experiences in the glory of God, we need to remember that most of life in God is not lived up there!

I want to experience everything God has for me, but if it doesn't happen exactly as I envision it, should I "dis" the church and the leaders? Do I stop attending? Should I go and try to start the extreme church of my dreams? Do I start rebelling against the norm because I don't like the feeling I'm getting?

I'm Bored!

You cannot measure the fullness of your life by the number of thrilling experiences you have. Parents need to live this out and teach their children that it is okay to be bored! Yes, I said bored! People need to learn how to live on *this* plane of life, too.

One day, I walked into our church foyer before service and found three little girls quietly sitting there. I asked them what they were doing. One of them replied, "Just sitting here being bored."

I asked, "How is that going?"

With a huge smile, she answered, "My Dad told us to sit here, be bored, and be happy about it, and that's what we are doing." I laughed, but I appreciate a father that would do that. I'm sure it was pure torture for them to sit and do nothing, but it was a great lesson to learn and they were passing it with flying colours. How awesome!

God never intended life to be a constant rush of fast-paced living, designed to continually titillate the senses. We need to take time to slow down, think, contemplate, relax, and be still. It seems that people are losing the ability to simply sit still. After five minutes, they are already screaming for something to do. I understand that we are living in a sight and sound generation that produces a need for constant amusement, but we must learn to live our lives within normal parameters. The problem is that many have no idea that this is an acceptable way of living. It's just too easy to say we are bored and give in to the need to experience something fast paced and heart thrilling.

I grew up listening to my parents tell stories of what Christmas was like when they were children. They didn't have all the stuff we have today, yet they spoke of Christmas as the most wonderful time of the year. It was a time when fun consisted of sleigh rides, skating on the pond, and making popcorn decorations for the tree. They visited with family by talking and listening to one another. Yes, they interacted with one another! They didn't have access to movies, Internet, Play Stations, Netflix, or other fantasy related paraphernalia, and yet they were very happy. What would happen if we tried to have Christmas the old-fashioned way today? Would there be a revolt? What my parents did in their day would seem slow, dull, or boring to the average person who grew up with a Nintendo controller in their hand. In fact, it is still this way when I visit my mother. She wants to spend time visiting, not watching television or playing video games, and she doesn't understand why her grandchildren want to do these things instead of talking with her. She might seem old-fashioned to many of us, but she certainly has a better grasp of reality. Too many are living out their lives in a fantasy world, and it is not beneficial. I think it's time to rethink what normal is, don't you?

GET REAL!

> *Better what the eyes see than wandering desire. This too is futile and a pursuit of the wind.* –ECCLESIASTES 6:9

REAL LIFE WILL NEVER LIVE UP TO OUR FANTASIES.

As Solomon aptly put it, it is better to enjoy what is right in front of us, than to have wandering desires that remain unfulfilled. People are so fantasy oriented that it is hurting their ability to enjoy what is real. I mean, what goes on in our minds is surely more exciting than reality. What is there in reality that can live up to what we can create in our minds? Real life will never live up to our fantasies. This is why books, movies, and the internet are all so popular. They create avenues to satisfy our adventure and pleasure seeking hearts and minds.

Pornography is such a strong addiction because it works in the mind to stimulate the pleasure centres in the brain. Porn has ruined many a marriage because the real thing becomes too boring or mundane in comparison to what goes on in a person's imagination. I believe this principle is at work in many areas of life, and its goal is to create dissatisfaction in people so they will seek greater extremes to satisfy that itch they cannot seem to scratch.

IF WE ADOPT A LIFESTYLE OF LOVING GOD,
SERVING HIM, AND REACHING OUT TO OTHERS,
OUR LIVES WILL NEVER BE DULL.

Drugs and alcohol are also tools used to desensitize people to the realities of life. Many became addicted to these substances at first because they seemed so fun, pleasurable, and satisfying, but that is a deception. The more they use, the less they are satisfied, creating the desire for more and more until only the extreme will do. Many substance abusers struggle with the concept of normal life because their minds are so messed up. Substances have hyped up their life so much and for so long, that the idea of normal is simply too dull. The truth is that no substance on earth can truly give the satisfaction we all crave. Reality is so much better than the deceptive, external influences offered today. Taking it a little further, only Jesus can give us what we really need to be happy and content! If we adopt a lifestyle of loving God, serving Him, and reaching out to others, our lives will never be dull.

EXTREME CHURCH

How has this extreme thinking affected the church? As the X-Y generations search for answers to their experience dilemma, they begin to look at the church, believing it to be the problem and, therefore, in need of elimination. As fantasy becomes the plumb line for the truth in our lives, it creates a thrust to change everything to match it. In an effort to resolve this quandary, coffee bars are installed, popcorn is served, sermons become shorter, music is redefined, and what was simply known as the prophetic is now *extreme* prophetic.

Now, I am not against the prophetic. God knows we need the gifts of the Spirit to be in operation, but why can't it just be done normally? What was wrong with just the prophetic? Why must it be *extreme* prophetic? Do we now teach God's gifts as extreme? What does *extreme tongues and interpretation* sound like? Do we need *extreme* dancing, shouting, singing, worshipping, jumping, or preaching? I don't know about you, but I can't extreme jump! My legs can only jump so high. Have we gone so far that spiritual normal is not good enough? Must it be extreme?

All of these changes are designed to incite a rush so that church can be exciting once again, but will it work? Is the changing of externals the answer? If we jump or dance a little higher or longer, will it truly bring the change we desire?

In recent times, I have heard from a variety of people all claiming to have a revelation of what the church needs today to keep it vital and thriving. Some say home groups are the way to go, while others say we should eliminate leadership altogether. Still others want the apostles to run things, and there are those who believe a return to the book of Acts church structure is the answer. Should we mimic first century believers? Will it bring about all that God wants to do in the earth? I can obviously see where some changes will be beneficial, but I struggle with blaming church structure for the lack of God's power on the earth.

SHUFFLING THE DECK

> THE MAIN PROBLEM IS NOT THE
> CHURCH ITSELF, BUT THE HEART.

The main problem is not the church itself, but the heart. If the heart is cold, or lukewarm towards God, or the things of God, will a structural change really fix it? Remember, the church is only as good as the people in it. Let me give you an example using an ordinary deck of cards. The cards represent the members of a church. If we were to take that deck and shuffle the cards, have we not successfully restructured them? Yes, we have, but have the cards themselves changed in any way? Did the queen now become the king? Did the two become the three? Shuffling the deck does essentially restructure it but is it not still the same deck as before? Would the old, well-used nine of diamonds suddenly become new and shiny again? Does submitting that card to a structural change affect the overall appearance or nature of it? No!

I do think people are looking for change because they've been disappointed in church, or they seriously do want to experience God's presence and power. On some level, these are both real and valid points; however, structural change will not fix the root of the problem. Granted, changes are definitely needed within the church, but if the hearts of the people don't change, aren't we merely shuffling the deck? This is why we need a revival in the people of God. As our hearts are revived, healed, and delivered, it won't matter what structure is in place. Don't be deceived; God is more interested in great hearts, love, and unity than He is in the structure of things.

IDENTITY CRISIS

People in today's society are in the process of creating a new normal—a lifestyle that fits their identities. As believers who have been translated from the kingdom of darkness into His light, we no longer fly under the banner of this world, no matter what passes as popular or prevalent culture. We are born anew into the culture and influence of our God, and we don't have to do anything extreme, different, or worldly, in order to have an identity.

When I was fifteen years of age, I wanted to fit in, so I followed the crowd and had my ear pierced. It is amazing what we will do to our bodies in order to identify with our peers. The problem was that I didn't like wearing it. It was uncomfortable and irritating. After some time, I stopped wearing it. Why did I do it? What was the big deal? What did I think to gain? I was giving in to the warped idea that if I did what was popular, I would suddenly be cool and accepted. What was new in the 70s is commonplace today. It seems that everyone has an earring or two.

When I was a teen, I asked my father for a pair of leather, squared toed boots. You know—the kind that bikers wore. I thought they were the most impressive footwear ever created. I remember it vividly when he called my name and said he had purchased the boots for me. I ran into the room with great anticipation and excitement and ripped them from his hand. To my surprise, they were boots, but they lacked the qualities aforementioned. Instead of leather, they were plastic, and to make matters worse, they had fur inside! Not only were they fake, they were winterized. Their only redeeming quality was they were square toed. I told my father, "There is no way on God's green earth I am ever going to wear those fake, fur lined boots!" Thus began the war. We fought about those stupid boots for the next hour. The rest of my family cleared away as the yelling and swearing began. We both stood our ground, adamantly refusing to back down. I stormed from the house in a rage, and he hollered after me that I would get nothing the next time. When I look back on those times, I think, *Why did I react in such an ungrateful and horrible manner?*

Fast-forward to when I first received Jesus as Lord and my life was completely transformed. Oh, what a change of heart I had! No longer did I require external hardware jutting from my body to feel good about myself, or fit in with the latest cultural standards. Jesus became my identity and life.

Can't get No ... Satisfaction!

Today's generation is constantly leaning towards the extreme in life. We no longer seem to be satisfied with what is deemed normal. People jump from one thing to another, all in the hopes of finding that ever-elusive satisfaction in life. I think what is happening in the world is being transferred into the church. While we must be ever changing to follow the Lord, it's important to remember that extreme thinking is at the root of some of these problems.

"*Treacherous, reckless, swollen with conceit, lovers of pleasure rather than lovers of God*" (2 Timothy 3:4, ESV). The problem behind the extreme church is its desire for pleasure. People who are pleasure seekers will certainly struggle with the church in its current state. It will be far too boring for their liking, and they will think, *The church needs to change!* However, this is not cause for change. We desire to be entertained, instead of being the ones who entertain God. Revelation 4:11 says we were designed for His pleasure, not Him for ours! The church must not allow itself to be so absorbed in its own pleasure seeking that it loses sight of what serving the Lord is all about and brings no honour and glory to God. Being normal is part of life, and we must not try to redesign it to satisfy our carnal appetites for pleasures and thrills.

I'm all for change. It is necessary, but it must be done for the right reasons and not motivated by the extremes of the thrill-seeking believer. If we are going to create a new normal, let's redefine it as the church giving all honour, glory, and praise to the King of kings and Lord of lords, who is deserving of all we can give. Let nothing be done for our own pleasure or satisfaction, but in obedience to the Word of God that exhorts us to do all for the glory of our Lord and Master, Jesus Christ, *"...to Him be glory in the church and in Christ Jesus to all generations, forever and ever. Amen"* (Ephesians 3:21).

4.

SPIRITUAL TEENAGERS

*... until we all reach unity in the faith and in the knowledge of God's Son, growing into a mature man with a stature measured by Christ's fullness. Then we will no longer be little children, tossed by the waves and blown around by every wind of teaching, by human cunning with cleverness in the techniques of deceit. But speaking the truth in love, let us grow in every way into Him who is the head—Christ. –*EPHESIANS 4:13–15

I remember being in the third or fourth grade, and the principal, Mr. Popick, was frowning as he caught me doing something foolish (a common occurrence). As he shook his head, he said, "Rudoski, Rudoski, if you had a brain, you'd be dangerous!" That being one of my fonder memories as a mischievous young lad; I can quite honestly say growing up was not an easy thing for me. According to my mother and her abundance of childhood stories, it appears that I spent as much time as possible getting into trouble and being immature. I vividly remember my Dad looking down at me with a perplexed expression that said, *What's wrong with that boy?* Catching me with a Tonka truck high over my head, about to pummel my cousin with it, or discovering me totally naked in the middle of the road, challenging the gravel trucks to a duel, caused my parents to shake their heads in bewilderment. At any rate, if I were ever left alone, even for the shortest time, trouble was sure to follow.

As I grew into my teen years, I continued to do some extremely stupid things. It's no wonder my father rarely gave me the keys to the car! Growing up was an ever elusive concept that seemed just beyond my grasp. One minute I could be hard working, responsible, and seemingly mature; only to do something incredibly childish the next. I don't know what it is about maturity that makes it so hard to achieve. Is it being more responsible, letting go of old thinking, or maybe, just maybe, we don't want to be mature? In any case, growing up is hard to do. A good friend of mine has a saying that I can agree with: Men don't grow a brain until they are thirty. We men might not want to hear that, but I can imagine all the women are nodding in agreement. Why do girls appear to mature more quickly than boys?

> We proclaim Him, warning and teaching everyone with all wisdom, so that we may present everyone mature in Christ. I labor for this, striving with His strength that works powerfully in me.
> —Colossians 1:28–29

It becomes quite apparent, after a careful reading of Paul's Epistles, that maturity is one of his recurring themes. This idea was ingrained into all the Jews of that day. They believed and taught that maturity was the end of Torah, meaning the fulfillment of it.

While many believers today, me included, want to major on miracles, signs, wonders, and supernatural acts of God, we must never lose sight of this very important part of God's plan for His people—that they mature in Christ. I am writing this to try to counter the spiritual immaturity that seems so prevalent in the church. We have majored on miracles, signs, wonders, and healing, but minored on character, growth and maturity. We get excited when a person is born again, and we spend so much time with them as babes in Christ. Then we see them grow a little, get some understanding, become card carrying members of the church, and we kind of forget about them, believing they are now mature. Yes, they may have experienced some growth, but are they fully developed and spiritually mature? In Paul's words, "... until we all reach unity in the faith and in the knowledge of God's Son, growing into a mature man with a stature measured by Christ's fullness" (Ephesians 4:13).

> JUST AS TEENAGERS CAN FALSELY ASSUME THEY ARE ALL
> GROWN UP BECAUSE THEIR BODIES HAVE DEVELOPED,
> SO WE CAN MAKE THE SAME MISTAKE SPIRITUALLY.

Many believers stop growing once they get to the adolescent stage in their spiritual life, thinking they are mature. Just as teenagers can falsely assume they are all grown up because their bodies have developed, so we can make the same mistake spiritually.

In this chapter, we want to deal with the issues, characteristics, and problems resulting from what I call "spiritual teenagers." I believe rebellion can be a fruit of spiritual immaturity. There are many who were born again some years ago who now begin to think and act like a spiritual teen, manifesting teenage character traits, both good and bad. While there are many good qualities about being a teen, we want to zero in on the ones that cause trouble in the church today.

I don't write any of this to pick on people, but to help us all understand and grow past this stage and into the fullness of the measure of the stature of Christ, He being our example to emulate and follow.

TIME TO GROW UP

> *Flee also youthful lusts; but pursue righteousness, faith, love, peace with those who call on the Lord out of a pure heart. But avoid foolish and ignorant disputes, knowing that they generate strife. And a servant of the Lord must not quarrel but be gentle to all, able to teach, patient, in humility correcting those who are in opposition, if God perhaps will grant them repentance, so that they may know the truth, and that they may come to their senses and escape the snare of the devil, having been taken captive by him to do his will.*
> —2 TIMOTHY 2:22–26, NKJV

Now some might read this and think Paul is talking about sexual lust, but I doubt Timothy was struggling with pornography or the like. No,

Paul was encouraging Timothy, a young man, to let no one despise his youth, and to be an example of faith, love, patience, righteousness, and gentleness. In the first century, Jewish leadership began at the age of forty. It would have been a rare thing indeed for Timothy to be given such a position with the assemblies of believing Jews. Because of his young age, Paul was exhorting Timothy to flee all youthful tendencies, prove himself worthy of leadership and win the trust of those older than him. The context isn't teenage lust, but teenage character traits.

In 2 Timothy 2:14, Paul says, "*Remind them of these things, charging them before God not to fight about words; this is in no way profitable and leads to the ruin of the hearers*" and verse 23 says, "*But reject foolish and ignorant disputes, knowing that they breed quarrels.*"

Notice the context is about words, speech, and disputes. Even though he was young, Timothy was mature enough not to get involved with disputes and quarrels about religion, the Word, or unprofitable things that did not benefit the hearer.

Growing Pains

As a little boy, I recall lying in bed at night in great discomfort. My mother would come in and calm my fears saying, "It's just growing pains. You'll be fine. We've all had them." We all experience physical pain as our body grows, so it's logical to conclude that we will encounter difficulties as we develop spiritually. As it is in the natural, so it is in the spiritual—we don't understand why it's happening and would rather avoid it altogether, but that would result in stunted growth.

The greatest mistake we can make is to think like a teenager, who believes he is more mature than he really is. I would say this is a common occurrence. In the spiritual sense, here is how it can happen. We all know baby Christians, brand new to this life, who exhibit baby tendencies. They are up and down emotionally, stick anything (teaching) in their mouths, and they are, for the most part, easy to work with, even though they need a lot of attention and help. You know how babies are. They cry a lot, need attention, and constant approval, yet are so much fun to be around. Their innocence, zest for life, and strong desire to listen and learn, make for an exciting time for parents or spiritual leaders.

However, after a time of growth, something else surfaces—a teen. Yes, a teenager! I know just reading this gives some of you the shakes as you reach for the pill bottle, and I understand completely, having had three teens of my own. I know people who say one day they woke up and, wham, they had a stranger in their home—a teenager!

Their teenager, once a functioning member of the household, had become so different, and almost unrecognizable to them. What happened to their nice little boy or girl who was once so adorable, cuddly, and sweet? Overnight, these teens become legends in their own minds. They question everything, struggle with authority, and speak about any topic as if they have it all figured out. They believe they are smart and wise beyond their years. This same person, who, not long before, was part of the family, is now reclusive, spending greater amounts of time in their room or with others like themselves. Two-way conversations have been replaced with a new language consisting of grunts, groans, and painful expressions. They may speak clearly in order to extract money from the parent, but all other conversation is avoided. You used to be able to ask a question and get a straight forward, honest reply; now you receive a defensive and protected response. Being in the house is torture for them, unless it is for eating or sleeping.

As it is in the Natural; so it is in the Spiritual

When a person is first saved, they don't have all the answers, they are humble, and they're eager to learn. After awhile, they can manifest the "Dad doesn't know anything anymore" trait within the church. Where they once loved to hear the preacher, sit in service, and receive prayer, now they exhibit signs of a spiritual teen. They are sulking, having an attitude of knowing better than their elders and an overall disrespect for the church in general.

DADS TURN OUT ALL RIGHT – IN TIME!
Author Unknown

4 years: My Daddy can do anything.

7 years: My Daddy knows a lot, a whole lot.

8 years: Dad doesn't know quite everything.

12 years: Oh well, naturally Dad doesn't understand.

14 years: Dad? Hopelessly old fashioned!

21 years: Oh, that man is out-of-date; what would you expect?

25 years: He comes up with a good idea now and then.

30 years: Must find out what Dad thinks about it.

35 years: A little patience; let's get Dad's input first.

50 years: What would Dad have thought about it?

60 years: I wish I could talk it over with Dad once more.

Before we go further, let me say this. When I say spiritual teen, I don't mean you have been saved for thirteen to nineteen years. I have seen the traits of a spiritual teenager exhibited in both the young and old. It is likely we have all displayed the turbulent signs of spiritual immaturity at some point in our lives. Let's take a look at some youthful traits and try to find ourselves spiritually.

There are exceptions, but, typically teenagers:

• *Have all the answers*

I am somewhat amazed at the "wisdom" that flows from my daughters these days. They always seem to know more than I do. I mean, sometimes they speak to me as if I am the child and they are the parent! While they may sound all grown up, they have a lot to learn about life.

• *Don't like to be corrected*

For some reason, they see correction as an attack on their self-image, and they will go so far as to try and correct the corrector. Yes, while being corrected or challenged, they will begin to correct the one correcting them.

• *Shift the blame*

It wasn't my fault ... my sister did ... or she didn't. "I never" is a common phrase, which leads them to:

• *Struggle with taking responsibility*

They cannot or will not accept responsibility for anything. Of course, the mistake often made by parents is they believe their teens are more responsible than they actually are. The truth is that although they may have grown a bigger, more mature looking body, their character has yet to catch up.

• *Whatever you want them to do is a huge inconvenience for them*

I love my children, but the three of them were experts at trying to talk me out of whatever it was I was asking them to do. Later was always a better time to get it done. They always promised to do it at their convenience.

• *Always and never*

Teenagers say things like, "My parents never listen to me," or "They always disrespect me," or "I never get to..." Teenagers, being idealistic in nature, lack balance, and struggle to see life as it really is.

• *Like to eat junk food*

Sometimes when I'm feeling brave and courageous, I will ven-
ture into the place where my teenage daughters dwell. It can
be a scary trip as I may come in contact with some unmen-
tionables, but every time I look into their den, I see the same
thing—the ghost of junk food's past. Crammed into every
bag, basket, nook, and cranny, there are the familiar wrappings
of chips, chocolate bars, pop, and this is just what I can see.
Truthfully, I'm terrified to look into one of the dresser draw-
ers. It doesn't matter how many lectures, talks or label readings
take place, the teen must consume its daily quota of junk!

• *Struggle with offenses*

Teenagers, although wanting to maintain the appearance of
strength, are very easily hurt. We must be careful what we say,
even in jest, lest we hurt their very fragile ego and self-image.
After all, image is everything to them. Teenagers hate to look
bad in front of their peers. Embarrassment is an almost un-
forgivable offense.

Now, after reading these character traits of a teenager, do they not
resemble church people at times? Do they ever exhibit adolescent behaviour? Do they have all the answers, knowing more than the pastor,
leaders or elders? Do they hate to be corrected? Do they shift the blame
to someone else, saying, "You know this sermon sure would be good for
brother so and so"? Do they take full responsibility to do the work of
the ministry, or is it for the leaders only? Do they say, "Someone else
will surely do it? I don't have time?" Do they seem inconvenienced when
leadership asks for assistance either spiritually or naturally? "You know,
they (leadership) are *always*...They *never* let me talk...They don't respect my ministry gifts, etc...If I was the leader, I would *never*..." Very
idealistic indeed!

INSTEAD OF BEING A GOOD SHEEP, EATING THE NICE,
SWEET GRASS THAT A GOOD SHEPHERD GIVES, THEY
ARE LIKE GOATS THAT WILL LITERALLY EAT ANYTHING.

Some church people will eat anything, anytime, anywhere. Instead of being a good sheep, eating the nice, sweet grass that a good shepherd gives, they are like goats that will literally eat anything. I once caught a goat eating my jacket, and it only relented after we had a great struggle. Christians, too, are susceptible to listening to or reading spiritual junk food, which is tasty at the time, appeasing to self-absorbed and itchy ears, but of no value nutritionally to their spiritual health and well being.

What about being offended or embarrassed? How many older believers still struggle with offenses that happened years ago? They are still struggling with issues in relationships, money or life itself. When they should be teaching and helping others, they are still in need of constant approval. In other words, they still want to be fed milk.

PEER PRESSURE

I want to throw one more onto the pile. It is a teenager's propensity to listen to the wrong crowd. I remember, as a teen, walking downtown at night with my friends, who like me had the answers to life all figured out. We had nothing, but we walked and talked, believing ourselves to be wiser than Solomon, discussing everything from girls and parents to God and religion and, of course, the existence of UFOs! If someone agreed with our philosophies, then they could be our friend. If not, they were out of luck.

Is the church like this too? Would we rather listen to our peers, instead of the good, Godly people under whom He has placed us? Would we rather listen to the junk food peddling, anti-church writers of the day, or the God placed, Holy Spirit inspired preachers and teachers within the safe house of the church?

The first eight chapters of Proverbs are written from a father's heart to his son, and throughout the chapters, wisdom is given to help the son navigate through the treacherous waters of life: "*The fear of the Lord is the* beginning of knowledge; fools despise wisdom and discipline. Listen, my son, to your father's instruction, and don't reject your mother's teaching" (Proverbs 1:7–8).

The greatest mistake spiritual teenagers make is to reject the wisdom of those who have gone before them. Teenagers can have a very rough time growing in this time of maturity. The temptation is to see oneself as fully-grown or mature, no longer needing the advice or wisdom older ones can bring. Many stop here on their spiritual journey, deceiving themselves into thinking they are spiritually mature and able to handle and understand life.

The thinking process goes something like this. When I was young, I needed your help. Now that I'm older, I no longer need you. I'm mature now, and I don't need to go to church, hear the preacher or get prayer. I'm a big boy now—I do it! We can even start to believe the older crowd is dumb or irrelevant.

Look what happened to a young king who refused to listen to his elders and opted to hear the voice of his peers instead.

> *Then Rehoboam went to Shechem, for all Israel had gone to Shechem to make him king. When Jeroboam son of Nebat heard [about it], for he was still in Egypt where he had fled from King Solomon's presence, Jeroboam stayed in Egypt. They summoned him, and Jeroboam and the whole assembly of Israel came and spoke to Rehoboam: "Your father made our yoke harsh. You, therefore, lighten your father's harsh service and the heavy yoke he put on us, and we will serve you." Rehoboam replied, "Go home for three days and then return to me." So the people left. Then King Rehoboam consulted with the elders who had served his father Solomon when he was alive, asking, "How do you advise me to respond to these people?" They replied, "Today if you will be a servant to these people and serve them, and if you respond to them by speaking kind words to them, they will be your servants forever." But he rejected the advice of the elders who had advised him and consulted with the young men who had grown up with him and served him. He asked them, "What message*

do you advise that we send back to these people who said to me, 'Lighten the yoke your father put on us?'" Then the young men who had grown up with him told him, "This is what you should say to these people who said to you, 'Your father made our yoke heavy, but you, make it lighter on us!' This is what you should tell them: 'My little finger is thicker than my father's loins! Although my father burdened you with a heavy yoke, I will add to your yoke; my father disciplined you with whips, but I will discipline you with barbed whips.'" So Jeroboam and all the people came to Rehoboam on the third day, as the king had ordered: "Return to me on the third day." Then the king answered the people harshly. He rejected the advice the elders had given him and spoke to them according to the young men's advice: "My father made your yoke heavy, but I will add to your yoke; my father disciplined you with whips, but I will discipline you with barbed whips."

—1 KINGS 12:1–14

Rehoboam, son of Solomon, was the newly appointed king, and he refused the advice of the elders and listened to the words of his peers, which almost always leads to trouble. The impetuousness of youth caused them to believe they were smarter and wiser than their elders. The biggest deception young people can conceive in their minds is that they have an understanding of life that even older people don't have.

I wonder how many people have thought, *If I was the leader, or if I was in control, or if they ever gave me the chance, I would…* Now it is one thing to want to be a leader, but quite another when you are saddled with all the responsibility that comes with it. You cannot have one without the other. James tells us that no one should take it upon themselves to be a teacher of others, for it comes with greater accountability before the Lord. Better to sit back, listen, learn and grow wiser.

I write all this because I see spiritual teenagers rising up in the church, and they are using media to voice their thinking, opinions, and ideas to anyone who will listen. I once made this statement to the younger leaders in our church, "It is to your advantage to be silent when you are younger. Perhaps God will give you a platform on which to speak one day.

If you speak now, just because you can through social media, then perhaps God will not give you the platform later. If you want to speak, then be silent now. It could be you will speak now and forever hold your peace!"

Like 2 Timothy 2:22 says, we need to flee youthful passions and grow up into mature people in Christ, He being the measure we aspire to imitate. Pursue faith, love, peace, and righteousness and run from all divisive, arrogant, and empty talk. Run from any youthful tendencies in your life. Grow in the grace of the Lord Jesus Christ and let Him make you mature in every area of life.

As we allow the "growing pains" process, the maturity will become evident to all. As a result, the church can become the strong, powerful, and united community God has designed it to be—vessels to house His presence, power, and Word.

5

CLIMBING
THE LADDER OF
SUCCESS

For promotion comes neither from the east, nor from the west, nor from the south. But God is the judge: he puts down one, and sets up another. –PSALM 75:6–7, KJV

How long must I work in the nursery before I can do something else? I've been ushering for a long time, so when will I be promoted to something greater? I have been faithful for over a year now, can I preach? I'm new to this church, but I can sing, so can I join the band? How long do I have to serve before I get to do something important? These types of questions have been asked in churches by promotion-oriented individuals for years and lead me to ask some of my own. When did church become a corporate ladder for an individual to climb and gain success? Have people forgotten that promotion comes from God and not from man?

> I heard of a man who said to the preacher, "I want to sing in your choir." The preacher replied," But you don't belong here. Where do you have your membership?" He said, "I don't belong to any local church. I belong to the invisible church." The pastor said, "Then I suggest you join the invisible choir."
> Vance Havner[5]

Sometimes people rebel against the church and authority because they feel that they were unjustly passed over for positions, or that leadership doesn't recognize them and their gifts. Because they feel disrespected, they often stop attending church altogether, or they might choose to leave and find another place that is willing to give them the position they desire. You see; they were looking to man instead of God. John Burton explains, "If you think you can't fulfill your destiny because of controlling, uncaring pastors, you don't know God very well!"[6]

If you are truly called to a ministry position, God will make a way if you remain humble, submitted, and maintain a good attitude. If it doesn't happen according to your timetable, it doesn't mean it will never happen. God could very well be using the people above you to mould you into the person He wants you to be. Let the process do its work in you! Sometimes, jumping ahead of the plan lands you right back to the beginning. Always remember, there are no shortcuts with God.

QUALIFICATIONS FOR LEADERSHIP AND SERVANT MINISTRY

This saying is trustworthy: "If anyone aspires to be an overseer, he desires a noble work." An overseer, therefore, must be above reproach, the husband of one wife, self-controlled, sensible, respectable, hospitable, an able teacher, not addicted to wine, not a bully but gentle, not quarrelsome, not greedy—one who manages his own household competently, having his children under control with all dignity. (If anyone does not know how to manage his own household, how will he take care of God's church?) He must not be a new convert, or he might become conceited and fall into the condemnation of the Devil. Furthermore, he must have a good reputation among outsiders, so that he does not fall into disgrace and the Devil's trap. Deacons, likewise, should be worthy of respect, not hypocritical, not drinking a lot of wine, not greedy for money, holding the mystery of the faith with a clear conscience. And they must also be tested first; if they prove blameless, then they can serve as deacons. Wives, too, must be worthy of respect, not slanderers, self-controlled, faithful in everything. Deacons must be husbands of one wife, managing their children and their own households competently. For those who have served well as deacons acquire a good standing for themselves, and great boldness in the faith that is in Christ Jesus. —1 TIMOTHY 3:1–13

Having been in the tenuous position of working with the Lord to empower others in the work of the ministry, I've often sought the Scriptures to ensure the utmost success in releasing ministries, gifts, and other positions. What I find extremely frustrating is the total disregard of the qualifying instructions for ministry. Could it be that some are passed over for ministry positions because they have not yet qualified themselves for it? This isn't often spoken of, but is most likely the truth of the matter. As a leadership team, we have had occasions where we've had to remove some people from public ministry due to disqualifying circumstances in their lives. This is always a difficult task, but one which the Word of God expects us to carry out.

A number of years ago, when I was the Young Adults minister, a couple began attending our church. After a while, they were given the opportunity to be part of the praise and worship team. They also began meeting with me for counseling for some ongoing problems in their lives and home. I found counseling them to be extremely trying, because they never wanted to take any responsibility for their actions and always blamed something or someone else. After a period of unproductive counseling, combined with their unwillingness to change, we had to ask them to step aside from ministry. Immediately, they left our church, joined another, and were promptly given a prominent ministry position. Their new pastor never contacted us to see why they left. Needless to say, they weren't at that church for very long, either.

EARNING RESPECT

What you do speaks so loudly that I cannot hear what you say.
Ralph Waldo Emerson[7]

Not only do we need to show ourselves faithful, but we also need to be a great example to the body of Christ to earn the right to speak. People will certainly listen to you if they have respect for you. If you try to speak without first gaining their respect, they will only listen to part of what you say. If you want them to listen to everything, then you must earn it by living it out in front of them; otherwise, who you are will speak louder to them than all the Scriptures, ideas, or revelations you can give them.

Along with being an example to the body of Christ, leaders must also have proven themselves faithful to their own families.

> *One who manages his own household competently, having his children under control with all dignity. (If anyone does not know how to manage his own household, how will he take care of God's church?)* –1 TIMOTHY 3:4–5

This Scripture means that the parents have raised their children to be in submission, not by being a bully, using force or fear, but through a lifestyle that has been proven to effectively inspire Godly submission. If parents cannot lead their families in this manner, they will not be able to lead God's people any better. Thus, the Godly leading of one's family must be a qualification for leadership ministry. If their family doesn't line up, then the person must be overlooked at that time. It doesn't mean it will be permanent, but until things change, it has to be that way. I'm not trying to do an in depth study on ministry qualifications, but merely pointing out that God clearly has requirements. As Paul says, *"And let them also be tested first; then let them serve as deacons if they prove themselves blameless"* (1 Timothy 3:10, ESV, emphasis added).

MANY LEADERS AND POSITION-SEEKING
BELIEVERS HAVE DISREGARDED THE SCRIPTURES
TO FURTHER THEIR OWN AMBITIONS.

Paul, in writing to Timothy, his dear son in the faith, was giving him instructions on what the qualifications were to serve within the community of believers. First, they were to be tested, or proven, and if they passed that test, they were allowed to serve in a particular area. Many leaders and position-seeking believers have disregarded the Scriptures to further their own ambitions. God has placed a high standard upon those who serve in the local church, but it looks as if man has lowered that bar so anyone can get in.

People leave churches all the time looking for promotion. Worse yet, they can leave one church today and have a position in another one tomorrow. Needy pastors seem willing to allow almost anyone to do anything, just so their churches can operate or function in an area. They don't care where the person came from or why, and show little concern for their lack of faithfulness. We have disregarded the Word of God so that we can grow our churches and ministries, but I dare say, it has been to our detriment!

Has the church modeled success after the standard set by the business world? Is our faithfulness to where God has called us incumbent upon whether our personal dreams are fulfilled or not? Has the church been relegated to a stepping stone to recognition, fame, and fortune? Where is the accountability? Where is the heart to submit to Godly authority and leadership? Where is the humility that is so badly needed in the people of God today?

When a person leaves a church and goes elsewhere, there should be some type of protocol in place. If a person comes into a new assembly, he or she could be bringing all sorts of baggage with them that will ultimately affect the new congregation if not properly dealt with. Too often, there is no investigation and no accountability. The effects can be devastating to the body of Christ as a whole. Paul says, *"But now God has placed each one of the parts in one body just as He wanted"* (1 Corinthians 12:18).

Whatever happened to being called by God to a particular body? How can you just leave one and join another? It's not like applying for a new job. God has called you to a particular body, so maybe it's time to stay put, roll up your sleeves, and make it work. You can't be like the kid who doesn't like something, so he takes his bat and ball and leaves. We win or lose as a team! Running to another church may appear to resolve the issues, but it is a temporary fix at best!

Paul, speaking to the congregation in Corinth, goes on to explain that God leads a person to a specific church as He sees fit, obviously putting individual gifts together as necessary. Some have mistakenly taken this chapter of Corinthians out of context by applying it only to the greater body of Christ and not to the local church. Some believe they can jump from church to church as it suits their fancy, forgetting that God is willing and able to lead us to our proper place.

I am not saying that you can never leave a church, but if it does happen, do it with the blessings of leadership, and be prepared to take a back seat at the new place. This isn't about your personal successes or ambitions!

DON'T DISQUALIFY YOURSELF

> *Now the works of the flesh are obvious: sexual immorality, moral impurity, promiscuity, idolatry, sorcery, hatreds, strife, jealousy, outbursts of anger, selfish ambitions, dissensions, factions, envy, drunkenness, carousing, and anything similar. I tell you about these things in advance—as I told you before—that those who practice such things will not inherit the kingdom of God.*
>
> —GALATIANS 5:19–21

Notice what the Word is stating here! A person who has selfish ambition will not inherit the kingdom of God. Anyone who operates in this fleshly, carnal attribute will certainly not be approved for ministry of any kind.

GOD IS NOT IN THE HABIT OF PROMOTING FLESH!

The problem with selfish ambition is it stems from the wrong heart. It is not a heart of humility, but a heart that is self-serving. It wants to use the church as a stepping-stone to promotion. God is not in the habit of promoting flesh! God's Kingdom is not like the kingdoms of the world, where success must be gained, often at any price. Peter says, *"Based on the gift they have received, everyone should use it to serve others, as good managers of the varied grace of God"* (1 Peter 4:10). Never use the gifts God has given you as a means to your own personal promotion or recognition!

Proud people have a feeling—conscious or subconscious—that "This ministry is privileged to have me and my gifts." They focus on what they can do for God. Broken people have a heart attitude that says, "I don't deserve to have any part of this ministry." They know they have nothing to offer God except the life of Jesus flowing through their broken lives.

Nancy Leigh DeMoss[8]

IF YOU PINE AFTER THE MINISTRY, YOU ARE NOT READY FOR IT!

The person striving for personal ministry, public recognition, or promotion will disqualify himself from the very thing he seeks. The enemy will be given room to move if the motivations of our heart are misplaced. If you pine after the ministry, you are not ready for it!

We have been instructed to give no place or opportunity for the enemy's schemes to operate in our lives. A person can have a desire for ministry; that is a good thing, but the desire must not motivate you to do whatever it takes to get it. This ensures a pure ministry to God's people and is a protection to you.

I have had people tell me, "If I just act like I don't want it, then I will get it." Again, they miss the point! If God has called a person, then He can make it happen. They are trying way too hard to see it come to pass. In my life, I knew exactly when God called me and knew He would bring it to pass. I never had to pine for it or work hard to get it or be anxious about it. In fact, I had to be dragged into it, almost kicking and screaming. Why? I knew it would be costly, and the responsibility would be high. Sometimes the people striving for ministry don't grasp these concepts and have a fantasy idea of it. The reality of ministry is this—it is hard work, and it is costly.

CONFLICT OF INTEREST

But if you have bitter jealousy and selfish ambition in your hearts, do not boast and be false to the truth. –JAMES 3:14, ESV

The person striving for position or promotion falls prey to the deadly wiles of selfish ambition. This evil mindset has caused the downfall of many people, weakened strong churches, and sabotaged the advancement of the Kingdom of God. James tells us that selfish ambition is demonic and is a root of evil. Why? People who have selfish ambition see life from the perspective of what *they* can get out of it, almost a *look at me* mentality. People without it see life as God sees it. Selfish ambition creates a conflict of interest. Too often, it is this inner conflict that derails the true plans and purposes of God in people.

Wikipedia defines conflict of interest as: "A set of circumstances that creates a risk that professional judgment or actions regarding a primary interest will be unduly influenced by a secondary interest."[9]

We have all watched television shows where the lawyer or policeman is banned from working on a case where a relative or friend is involved. Their connection to the victim, or the accused, is referred to as a conflict of interest. Their emotional attachment produces an inability to see the truth of the matter, so in the interest of fairness and justice, they are removed from the case.

What does this mean in a ministry context? These secondary motives of recognition, fame, wealth, or prestige will undermine the purity of the minister and make him ineffective. In other words, the position becomes more about the person ministering than the people being ministered to, which should be the primary motivation. Taking this conflict away will help ensure pure ministry!

So many times, I have seen people fall prey to this insidious heart issue and then leave a perfectly good church to seek out their own ministry, all in the name of, *I just want to do more,* or *I don't feel fulfilled here* or *I am not recognized.* The problem seems to be the constant idea that unless a person has a position of prominence, they have not fulfilled God's calling. Nothing could be further from the truth!

> SOME PEOPLE JUDGE THEIR STATE OF
> HAPPINESS BY THEIR CURRENT MINISTRY
> PLACEMENT, POSITION, OUR FUNCTION.

Some people judge their state of happiness by their current ministry placement, position, or function. Somewhere along the way, they lost the joy of knowing Jesus and serving Him in whatever capacity needed. Christians often don't feel successful in their lives unless they have a full-time ministry position. What they will see one day is that true happiness can't be found in any of this; it can only be found in Jesus.

Too often I have heard this statement, "We left the church so we could do more." What they are really saying is that if they could get the position or promotion they desired, they could do more here, but since they haven't been released into it, they must go somewhere else to find it.

Here is another common statement, "We couldn't fulfill our calling there!" What are they saying? Does fulfilling your calling require position or prominence? Can't it be done without those titles or positions? Many have said they wanted to do more, but the sad reality is they will not go and do more; they might even end up doing less.

One of the major problems we are seeing in the church is people who are still following the *world's way of thinking* concerning success. They still believe the church is the place where they will climb the ladder of success. While this may be true for some, it isn't the truth for everyone. Some will be promoted in God's Kingdom to a full time ministry setting, but others won't. However, God wants to promote everyone in some way. Ministry is not the only way God promotes or repositions or blesses!

IN GOD'S KINGDOM, THE WAY UP IS DOWN!

In the church world, the way up is down, and the way down is up. I can also say it this way (if there is such a thing as the top): we don't rise to the top; we are called to it. Too many people think that if they have been in a church for a good number of years, it automatically puts them at the top of the list to move up the corporate ladder. This may work in the world, but not in the church. Now, while it is true that being faithful is a pre-requisite for many things in the church, not everything falls under its banner.

The truth is that the body of Christ is being weakened by this worldly way of thinking. We must renew our minds to the Word of God and start to do it His way. It's time to stop looking at the church we are in right now as our way to future success in ministry, and just serve the Lord wherever we can. If He wants to call us into a specific position or function, that is His prerogative, not ours. Our main calling is to be a contented sheep, stay happy, and serve wherever we are asked. We must not be deceived into thinking we should receive a position or placement as a result of our faithfulness or natural human qualities. After all, it is God who sets one up and puts down another.

CALLED AND CHOSEN

> Now there were in the church at Antioch prophets and teach-ers, Barnabas, Simeon who was called Niger, Lucius of Cyrene, Manaen a lifelong friend of Herod the tetrarch, and Saul.
> —ACTS 13:1, ESV

Notice where they were when they were called? They were in the church, submitted to authority, and serving via their fivefold ministry gifts. They didn't have to go and start their own church or become the number one guy to do this. They were working within the local church and then, and only then, did the Holy Ghost call them to go out and fulfill another work of ministry. This proves that yes, indeed, one can work as a minister with-in the local church body. In my years, I have seen many who were called to five-fold ministry, but were unwilling to operate in their gifting and func-tion within the local church. They all wanted to be the *man!* While this is certainly true of some, it is not true for everyone. The result is a lot more churches that are often weak in strength, resources, and effectiveness.

> While they were worshiping the Lord and fasting, the Holy Spirit said, "Set apart for me Barnabas and Saul for the work to which I have called them." Then after fasting and praying they laid their hands on them and sent them off. —ACTS 13:2–3, ESV

BASICALLY, THE WHOLE SYSTEM OF SENDING AND RELEASING
HAS BEEN SABOTAGED BY SELFISH PEOPLE WHO
DESIRE PERSONAL SUCCESS AT SOMEONE ELSE'S EXPENSE.

When it was time for Paul and Barnabas to go out, the Holy Ghost called them, and all the leaders were aware of it. The Holy Ghost didn't tell Paul and Barnabas they were to be set apart, and then fail to tell the leaders. It appears to me that everyone was working in unity. They were in agreement and all submissive to the Holy Ghost, and the ones being called out must have been in submission to the leaders. Then it says that they laid their hands on them and sent them out. This must be our clue as to the how, when, what, and why of sending people out in function and purpose. Again, we must not fall for the world's way of thinking. When and how it all works out isn't up to us. If God wants it to happen, it will, and all will know and see it. However, many people who go out and start ministries or churches don't do it this way. They feel dissatisfied or unfulfilled where they are, and finally go and do it, with no thought or care of what established authority has to say. Basically, the whole system of sending and releasing has been sabotaged by selfish people who desire personal success at someone else's expense.

Before I go on, I want to make mention of the many who have remained faithful, kept their hearts right, and haven't operated out of selfish ambition. These people are the heroes in any church! They have passed the test and proven themselves in God's eyes and are qualified for promotion. Not everyone who is faithful will get promoted into a position or ministry, but God will promote them in some way. You can bet on that.

SELFISH AMBITION

While everyone has different gifts and functions to serve God in the body of Christ, we're certainly not all called to the five-fold ministry. When people continue to strive for what they are not called to, problems will arise. I know people who were convinced they had a five-fold ministry calling, but the fact that it never came to pass was a constant source of dissatisfaction for them. They refused to recognize that they weren't called or anointed for the position they desired, and in the process they overlooked the very gifts that would make them successful in the Kingdom of God. They foolishly believed that if they could attain a certain position of ministry, contentment would surely follow. Instead of using the gifts unique to them, they spent time and energy trying to be something they were not. The end result was people who were unhappy with themselves, their church leaders, and ultimately, God Himself. Furthermore, because of positional dysfunction, the advancement of God's Kingdom is impeded.

> *This is not the wisdom that comes down from above, but is earthly, unspiritual, demonic. For where jealousy and selfish ambition exist, there will be disorder and every vile practice.*
> —JAMES 3:15–16, ESV (EMPHASIS ADDED)

Everyone is called to operate in faithfulness and serve without selfish ambition. What would the church look like if everyone had a heart to serve with humility? Selfish ambition has produced many of today's rebellious attitudes against church leaders. This essentially reduces spiritual leadership down to a means to further one's own agenda. The selfish will abuse spiritual leadership to gain promotion or position.

Selfish ambition is just another name for rebellion. Rebellion, at its very core, is the strong desire to do your own thing, regardless of what anyone else says. Rebellion refuses to listen to the wisdom of godly people already established in the corporate church. God has placed these people in the body as it has pleased Him. They didn't do it on their own. Some people who suffer with selfish ambition believe these people got there because of someone they knew, or the particular family they were born into. This is a deception, because it is God who sets one up and puts one down. God will work and who can stop Him?

TRUE HUMILITY

> *But the wisdom from above is first pure, then peaceable, gentle, open to reason, full of mercy and good fruits, impartial and sincere.* —JAMES 3:17, ESV

I love this verse! It really speaks to me about what our hearts should be like. These traits are in total opposition to the heart of rebellion. This wisdom is as pure as rebellion is impure. It is peaceable, gentle, open to reason, and willing to yield. These are the characteristics of true humility, and they are in direct contrast to the characteristics of rebellion. Rebellious people are *not* peaceable, willing to yield, or open to reason. They want their own way and will allow nothing or no one to hinder their plan, especially not seasoned leadership!

REBELLION WILL TRAMPLE ON THE WORD OF GOD TO ACCOMPLISH ITS OWN PURPOSES.

James also says, "impartial and sincere." What? Can you see it? Humility doesn't seek its own; it can see the truth because it has no selfish ambition attached to it. The heart of rebellion is selfish, and it cannot understand the heart of humility. Rebellion will trample on the Word of God in order to accomplish its own purposes. It has no concern for the truth and is only moved by selfish ambition. This idea has been the Petri dish of rebellion that has grown into an infection, manifesting itself in the church and inflicting great damage to the Kingdom of God. It is insidious, evil, and demonic. It must be eradicated! Humility is the antidote we all desperately need in order to spurn the malignant hold of rebellion.

HUMILITY IS THE ANTIDOTE WE ALL DESPERATELY NEED IN ORDER TO SPURN THE MALIGNANT HOLD OF REBELLION.

WILLINGNESS TO YIELD!

Yielding is where true humility really shines. People who are humble will yield to one another. They will be willing to listen to reason, and won't become contentious and stubborn. A person who is yielded both to God and man will be gentle, full of mercy, and produce good fruit. In other words, they will be known both for who they are, and how they live.

Some say, "I only listen to God." While this is "a truth" concerning the way God communicates with man, it is not the "the whole truth." God has given the gift of teaching and preaching as another way to speak to His people.

We are instructed over and over again to follow our leaders and submit to them. God works in conjunction with His ordained leadership and asks all of us to do the same. If you truly have a God given desire to be in ministry, then let godly conduct help you flow in the right direction. Why shipwreck your calling with a rebellious attitude? If you are truly called, you won't need to rebel to receive it or walk in it. Being yielded will produce the desired results, thus eliminating the need to rebel. Sometimes, I think the rebellious don't trust anyone and lack faith in God. Rebelling to get what we desire shows a lack of faith. We don't have to rebel to walk in God's promises.

I want to encourage you to keep a humble heart and not allow your own ambitions to cloud your true and proper understanding of the Kingdom of God and its operation. God alone is the one who promotes. Don't spend time going after what you want. Instead, go after the qualities of the heart that produce peace, humility, and willingness to yield to another, and you'll pull the rug right out from under the feet of rebellion. Be careful not to fall for the idea that the church is a corporate ladder to success. It may look like it from a distance, but it's not the same as the world. God is the one who promotes, and He is faithful to do it!

6

DISAPPOINTMENT'S
DECEPTION

Disappointment—what a horrible thing in a person's life! Imagine what goes on in people affected by its grip! Envision the discouragement, the disillusionment, and the heartache associated with disappointment. Imagine the hurt that comes and tries to wrap itself around the heart of the disappointed one! We have all felt its painful touch. The problem with being disappointed, if we don't learn to deal with it, is that it can be the catalyst for future rebellion. This is why we must teach people how to overcome disappointment and discouragement. Some of today's rebellion is the fruit of yesterday's disappointment!

SOME OF TODAY'S REBELLION IS THE FRUIT OF YESTERDAY'S DISAPPOINTMENT!

Disappointment creates a "change what is around me" mentality. If I'm disappointed, then something must change, and it is not going to be me. Disappointment, then, is a major motivator of rebellion. Let's look at this dastardly *D* word, and see if we can get some understanding, revelation, and help.

Disappointment happens to all of us at varying degrees throughout life. We don't always deal with it correctly, nor do we understand the who, what, or why of it. Life does not guarantee that every day will be a walk in the park. Disappointment has a chance to touch us at every twist and turn we take. It has no concern or compassion for its victims. Its mark is clearly seen, heard, and felt among the populace. No one has escaped disappointment's tug or grasp. No one can say, "I will never be disappointed!"

I can vividly remember when I was first introduced to Jesus. Many people told me that because I was a Christian, everything I ever dreamed or desired would now come to pass. They claimed that life would be a proverbial bed of roses. However, there was a discrepancy between what people said and what actually happened in my life. Disappointment definitely came to me, and the crisis brought me to a crossroads where I had to make a decision. Would I continue to love and serve the Lord faithfully even when things didn't go my way? Should I go on when I had such disappointment in my heart? Is this the way it is going to be from now on? These questions and more plagued me at every turn, until I came to the realization that I must love and serve God no matter how disheartened I became. I chose to serve the Lord even if He never did anything for me again. Obviously, God has continued to do amazing things in my life since then, but my attitude will always reflect that understanding. In Proverbs we read, *"Delayed hope makes the heart sick, but fulfilled desire is a tree of life"* (Proverbs 13:12).

Disappointment rears its ugly head in a wide variety of ways and methods, the most common being when the thing we desire is delayed or doesn't happen. Perhaps we haven't achieved the job or career we desired, or marriage doesn't seem to bring the happiness we thought it would. What happened? Isn't marriage supposed to be the happiest thing in life? I'm amazed to find that people are getting divorced for the very same reason they got married—to be happy!

DISAPPOINTED IN CHURCH

Some people want to change everything about church because they were hurt in it. Their thinking goes like this: *I got disappointed in church; therefore church must be wrong, and it is up to me to fix it. God must not be in it anymore, for if He were, I certainly would be much happier, and I wouldn't be wounded.* Because disappointment has stolen our happiness, we lash out at the system called church. In our efforts to bring the church back in line, we think we must retaliate with rebellion. If we are to be content in church, then we must, out of necessity, change it all. This unspoken thought process has surely led to much of the ongoing rebellion within the church.

YOU CAN'T HAVE A HURTING HEART AND STILL HAVE A HEALED OUTLOOK.

Disappointment has the power to affect the condition of the heart, and we all know that out of the heart come the issues of life (Proverbs 4:23). In plain English, the condition of our heart affects what we see, feel, and think, which in turn influences our decisions. Whatever your heart is like, so will your life be! The two are intertwined like conjoined twins; one cannot move without the other. You can't have a hurting heart and still have a healed outlook. If the heart is affected, it will be manifested in your life. Disappointment, at its very root, begins to distort the way we see everything. Much of what is outwardly manifested as rebellion is just the overgrown fruit of a disappointed heart.

> *"The kingdom of God is like this,"* He said. *"A man scatters seed on the ground; he sleeps and rises—night and day, and the seed sprouts and grows—he doesn't know how. The soil produces a crop by itself—first the blade, then the head, and then the ripe grain on the head. But as soon as the crop is ready, he sends for the sickle, because the harvest has come."* —MARK 4:26–29

The parable of the sower and the seed is well known to most of us who have been in the Kingdom for any length of time, and it yields a great deal of understanding about how the heart works. While I'm not trying to teach a course on the heart, it is certainly worth considering.

The seed represents the Word of God, or words, and the ground speaks of the heart of man. Just as natural seeds go into the ground and begin to grow, words spoken begin to grow or take root in the heart (spirit) of man. I want you to pay particular attention to the phrase, *"the soil produces a crop by itself."* The heart does something very unusual; it works on causing growth to come to whatever has been deposited there.

73

It doesn't differentiate between the good seed and the bad; it just continues to work on that seed. Even if we deny it, it still does its designed task.

Fence Posts

One time, I was pulling out an old fence so I could build the new one. As I dug it out, I noticed that each of the posts had substantially decayed below ground. This was hardly noticeable on the portion above ground. From the time those posts were first pounded into the ground, the soil has been trying to accomplish what God intended—cause whatever was placed there to grow. The decay was a direct result of the soil's God-given assignment to cause the growth of whatever is put in it. Soil produces a crop all by itself, needing nothing to aid it, except seed.

Now what does this have to do with disappointment, you ask? You see, when the heart is affected by disappointment, it takes that seed and tries to make it grow. And grow, it does! Disappointment, left to fester in the heart of man, will continue to grow and get stronger. That is why it is so vital to look after what is in our hearts. We can't always stop what gets pushed in there by the hardships of life, but we most certainly can do something about whether it remains and is allowed to take root and grow.

Yesterday's Disappointments = Tomorrow's Rebellion

The heart of the wounded often cries out for justice, judgment, or change. If it isn't healed, it can be the catalyst for the root of rebellion. A great deal of the rebellion found in the church world is merely the fruit of disappointment ripening on the vine of our hearts.

> A great deal of the rebellion found in the church world is merely the fruit of disappointment ripening on the vine of our hearts.

A great deal of rebellion's fruit stems from the disappointments of life. This can motivate a person to look to change something, often by whatever means necessary. However, while the change may seem like the natural outflow of the heart, it's not the proper response. A person may be operating out of a rebellious heart and be oblivious to it. In some cases, the perpetrator is totally unaware of the condition of his own heart.

Am I saying that change is wrong? Absolutely not, but all change must be accompanied by the right attitude if it is to be effective. Anything born out of a disappointed heart will only produce more disappointment. Change can be a good thing, and it is needed in life, as is justice, and even judgment, at times. However, anything done for the wrong reason will only cause more trouble.

Out of the heart flow the forces of life, and that's what we base our daily decisions on. If we allow fear to rule, then fear will be the result. In fact, any hurtful emotion that leads us to make a decision out of a wrong heart will only bear bad fruit. Everything produces fruit after its own kind, both good and bad, naturally and spiritually. Fear only produces more fear; anxiety produces anxiety, anger, more anger, and so on. It is the cycle of life flowing out of the heart of man.

IS YOUR VIEW ASKEW?

The prolonging of what we hope for has an adverse effect on the heart and mind of man. The "heart" is simply what is going on inside of a person. It is the core of the individual. Whether we admit it or not, disappointment negatively impacts our outlook on life, and we need to guard our hearts very diligently.

...OUR PERCEPTION INFLUENCES OUR OUTLOOK.

Hope deferred affects the eyesight of the heart. I heard a story about a man who sat at the kitchen table and complained continually to his wife about how dirty their next-door neighbours were. He thought their house, vehicle, and yard were just filthy. Day after day, he commented about it until one time he looked out the window and noticed a marked improvement. To his wife, he exclaimed, "The neighbors must have cleaned it all up!"

"No," his wife answered, "I just cleaned our window!" That's a funny story, but it is a great depiction of how our perception influences our outlook. The problem wasn't the people living beside him; it was his perception of them. He had come to the conclusion they were just dirty people, but the real dirt was in *his* heart. Because of his marred view, he couldn't see anything clearly; therefore, his vision of everything was askew.

How often has the pain of disappointment and hurt initiated rebellion? How many times have we lost sight of the reality of life as a result of a hurting or wounded heart? Is it possible that we are trying to change something, not because it is the right thing to do, but because we can't see clearly with our heart so sick from disappointment?

David is an excellent example of how to keep the root of rebellion out of a disappointed heart.

> *David and his men arrived in Ziklag on the third day. The Amalekites had raided the Negev and attacked and burned down Ziklag. They also had kidnapped the women and everyone in it from the youngest to the oldest. They had killed no one but had carried them off as they went on their way. When David and his men arrived at the town, they found it burned down. Their wives, sons, and daughters had been kidnapped. David and the troops with him wept loudly until they had no strength left to weep. David's two wives, Ahinoam the Jezreelite and Abigail the widow of Nabal the Carmelite, had also been kidnapped. David was in a difficult position because the troops talked about stoning him, for they were all very bitter over the loss of their sons and daughters.*
> —1 SAMUEL 30:1–6a

It is amazing to me how these guys who were being healed of their problems through their association with David, were now, by virtue of their disappointed hearts, speaking of stoning him. What were they doing? They were contemplating rebellion against their leader, the man who had taken them in, accepted, and loved them when no one else would.

Disappointment tries to adjust to what is around it and compensate for the pain it is feeling, but it tries to fix what it sees through the wrong channels. People are prone to lash out when they have been disappointed, usually holding the authority figures in their lives responsible for their pain.

Hope delayed makes the heart sick! Disappointment can have a powerful effect on one's emotional state. It can cause the strongest of people to do the craziest things, and turn the faithful into the unfaithful in a split second.

Rebellion tends to attack the one it believes responsible for the pain and disappointment. Rebellion is the natural offspring of a distorted viewpoint of the disappointed heart! While we expect such behaviour in the world, it is becoming far too common in the church world. Once disappointment settles on some church folk, who would have happily followed their leaders anywhere, they begin to think and act in a rebellious manner.

DON'T ATTACK!

> But David found strength in the Lord his God. David said to Abiathar the priest, son of Ahimelech, "Bring me the ephod." So Abiathar brought it to him, and David asked the Lord: "Should I pursue these raiders? Will I overtake them?" The Lord replied to him, "Pursue them, for you will certainly overtake them and rescue the people." –1 SAMUEL 30:6b–8

Notice what David did not do: he did not attack God, God's leaders, God's people or God's Kingdom in retaliation for his disappointment! Instead, the Bible says he strengthened himself in the Lord. He did not lash out at anyone, nor did he become rebellious in his efforts to ease the pain of the disappointment he was experiencing. David did what a lot of us don't; he sought after God, who helped him think, see, and respond correctly. God continued to mould David into the great king he would soon be. David turned disappointment into a great victory!

A wrong response here would surely have jeopardized his future as king. The way we deal with disappointment is crucial. Our response will either fortify our future or put it in jeopardy. If we allow a root of rebellion to grow out of our disappointments, we can literally kiss a good and godly future good-bye. God refuses to endorse rebellion! He is not the author of rebellion of any kind.

Disappointments in life are devastating to us. Our fragile, utopian mindsets struggle to comprehend the pain and disillusionment created by life's disappointments.

Adults rebel against established authority, usually God first, then authority of some kind, be it spiritual or natural. Children can rebel against their parents, the ones who love them the most and desire good things for them. People rebel against the establishment, thinking there has got to be a better way. Have you ever thought something like this: *If I was the pastor, I would do it this way, or if I was the boss, I would …?*

> WE CANNOT BE A CHURCH BUILT PRIMARILY ON
> REBELLION AGAINST THE THINGS WE DO NOT LIKE!

We cannot be a church built primarily on rebellion against the things we do not like! Many governments have been toppled by the ideals of the rebel, who believed his way was the only correct one. Adolph Hitler used his disappointments to fuel his own rebellion, and look where he ended up. He committed suicide when he saw his rebellious empire crumbling. The Nazi party started out as a minority and grew when rebellion asserted its voice. The problem with rebellion is that it continues to produce after its own. Rebellion creates more rebellion!

Disappointment can lead a person to think such thoughts as, *This is not the reality I signed up for, therefore; it must not be right. If I am in so much pain, how can this be right?* So the lashing out begins! We start to analyze and rethink all we have previously been taught, and our inner revolution is birthed. We question and doubt what is going on in our lives, and usually end up attacking the structure of established authority, which we perceive to be the obvious source of our disappointments.

> DISAPPOINTMENT HAS BECOME THE JET
> FUEL FOR A POWERFUL TWENTY-FIRST
> CENTURY REBELLION IN THE CHURCH.

Many, many people have left the church as a result of disappointment. If I am disappointed, then the church must be wrong ... or so their thinking goes. They opt out and start looking for a better solution, not realizing the problem is not outward, but inward. How many books attacking the church have been, or currently are being, written? Disappointment has become the jet fuel for a powerful twenty-first century rebellion against the church. A lot of good and sincere believers are being led down the garden path by the disappointments they have experienced while in the church. Many disappointed people have become modern day prophets who are declaring an anti-church message borne out of their hurts. Many are using the platform of social media to speak from their hurting hearts. Rebellion will never make the wounded heart whole again.

Many disappointed people have become modern day prophets who are declaring an anti-church message borne out of their hurts.

DOWN WITH THE MAN

I'm reminded of the disappointments and struggles young people faced in the 1960s and 70s. It seemed as if they couldn't come to terms with the Vietnam War, the man, or the establishment. They thought, *If this is the end result of all that is good and holy, then why bother. If the value system of this current generation results in my disappointment, then those values must be declined for higher ones that make me happy.* That, my friends, was the motivation for rebellion.

They felt the established structure must be the problem, so they lashed out by living a counter lifestyle, and tried to change the very fabric of the nation. The effects of their rebellion are still felt today. Suddenly, there was a lack of values as many young people embraced the ideology of freedom at the expense of personal responsibility. Instead of a love for government, city and country, there was an over-emphasis on self-love, leading to a "you can't tell me what to do generation." This was very different from the life portrayed on *My Three Sons, Leave it to Beaver,* or *Little House on the Prairie.* The question put forward because of disappointment is this, "If this is right, why does it feel so wrong?"

People assume that if we do everything properly, then life will turn out correctly. We must remember that we exist in a world still influenced by many factors, not all of them good. We live in a fallen world with fallen people who make fallen mistakes. While Jesus has paid the price and redeemed this world, including its rebellious nature, the fullness has not yet been seen. We must also be aware that, in the midst of all of our disappointments, God is still there for us.

We want to blame God, but we know that is the wrong thing to do, so we attack what we can—established authority. Most rebellion toward established authority in our lives has one thing at its root—*disappointment*.

Instead of looking to ourselves in self-examination, we look to shift the blame to the external. After all, I certainly couldn't be the problem, could I? Examining our lives periodically would do us a lot of good and just might save us all a lot of trouble.

It is the baby in us that fights and fusses when things don't go our way. Babies get their way for a time until the training process kicks in. It's not easy, but if they aren't taught, children will look to outsource the blame. Eventually, they will point the finger at their parents, so they must learn early on that there isn't always an explanation for their disappointments. No one is immune to the struggles life brings. Some never learn how to deal with disappointment, but it is extremely important that we do. If you are a parent, teach your children how to handle disappointment. Don't let it affect them and control their emotions and outlook. Teach them that life can be disappointing at times, but they serve a God who always causes them to triumph in Christ. Help them stay positive and continue to hope in God.

LET'S GO BACK TO DAVID. DAVID DID
NOT BLAME ANYONE—NOT GOD, HIS
PEOPLE, OR THE ESTABLISHMENT

David and his men lifted up their voices and wept, but nothing changed for the better until he sought out the Lord for direction and encouragement. David did not blame anyone—not God, His people, or the establishment! The mature seek the Lord for wisdom and guidance; the immature want to shift the blame to the establishment or leadership.

We can't rebel against everything just because we have been disappointed. David stayed humble and submissive throughout his disappointments. He never faltered in character or loyalty to the Lord, the King, or the people of God. He did not lash out in frustration because life wasn't going his way. In fact, David shows us quite the opposite. He had a heart after God that didn't change because of disappointing events or circumstances. David didn't allow disappointment to control his heart, and he stopped rebellion dead in its tracks. His thoughts and actions remained godly and sound. He did not fear, lose courage, or lose his head. He kept himself pure before the Lord and to His purposes. David went to God, humbled himself and asked for wisdom, and God gave it. Because of that wisdom, they recovered everything that was stolen. There was no need to let disappointment grow in his heart, and there was no need to change what was established. There was simply no need to rebel.

David manifested the characteristics that qualified him to be chosen by God as the future king of Israel. I can't imagine what would have happened had he rebelled against God. What was this character trait that defined David as a true king and servant of the Lord? What caused him to remain true and steadfast in the midst of severe rejection and disappointment? He was a man after God's own heart; he strengthened himself in the Lord and refused to give in to disappointment. A man after God's heart is not a rebel, for God is not rebellious!

> We know that all things work together for the good of those who love God: those who are called according to His purpose. For those He foreknew He also predestined to be conformed to the image of His Son, so that He would be the firstborn among many brothers. –ROMANS 8:28–29

Have we forgotten what the Lord is doing? His plan is to see good in our lives, and His purpose is not only to take us through, but continue to mould us into His own image and likeness. We don't just get through situations; we are remade into His image during the process. God hasn't merely saved us, but has recreated us to be like His only begotten Son. We are being transformed into the very essence of who God is.

We need to remember that it is only when we live according to His purposes that all things work out in our favour. We may be disappointed because things are not developing as we had planned, but we are still the clay, not the potter. God is the potter who works to change the disappointments in our lives into something incredible if we allow Him the chance to do it, and keep our hearts right during the process. If we continue to be guided by disappointment, we inspire our hearts toward rebellion and become the potter instead of the clay. We are to stay soft and pliable when disappointment knocks on the door of our hearts. God will even cause the disappointing things to work for our good.

DISAPPOINTMENT DIVIDES

SATAN WANTS DESPERATELY TO SEPARATE US FROM GOD. HE USES THE DISAPPOINTMENT WE STRUGGLE WITH AS A TOOL TO TRIGGER THINKING THAT IS CONTRARY TO HIS WORD.

Satan wants desperately to separate us from God. He uses the disappointment we struggle with as a tool to trigger thinking that is contrary to God's Word. Just like he did with Eve, the enemy of our souls tries to get us to believe God is somehow holding out on us. He wants us to suppose God isn't as good as He says He is and that a disappointed life is all there is. The devil's intention is to convince us that life is futile and that God is a million miles away, not caring or wanting to help us. He wants us to take matters into our own hands and not fully trust in God to let His perfect will work in our lives.

Do not look at what hasn't happened; rather, look at what God is doing and who He is making you into. Don't focus on the disappointing things in your life. Let them be stepping-stones into something great. God did it for David, and He will also do it for you and me.

IN THE MINISTRY

I have been in church and ministry for twenty-eight years at the time of this writing, and I've had plenty of opportunities to allow the disappointments of life to derail me. If you won't rebel, but stay faithful and loyal to the people God has asked you to submit to, He will take every adversity and turn it around for your good. I have seen God do this in my life time and time again, but there is a price to pay. It is the cost of keeping my heart clean before God and man. When we rebel, we unwittingly move in the spirit and direction of Satan. He is the initiator of all rebellion known on the earth, and he wants all of us to copy his evil ways. We must resist the desire to rebel against authority, and instead, submit, not only when things are good, but also when they aren't very pleasant. As you do, you will reap a harvest of good and godly fruit.

WHAT CAN WE DO?

Proverbs 4:23 tells us to *"guard your heart above all else, for it is the source of life."* If our heart becomes disappointed, the vines of darkness, disease, and even death can begin to grow. Disappointment is one vine we cannot afford to allow to mature in our hearts, as it will destroy us and those we do life with. Heart issues left unresolved don't just affect the one who has them, but they reach out to everyone around.

Determine that the giant of disappointment will not alter the heart you have for God, His Kingdom or His people. When disappointment comes, don't let it be the catalyst for rebellion. Instead of getting upset or picking up stones to throw at someone, be like David and go to God. David could have started throwing a few stones of his own, but he didn't. Instead, he did what Jesus would have done and put everything into the hands of God. He strengthened himself in the Lord by simply trusting in the God who had always proven Himself faithful.

If we allow disappointment to stay lodged in our hearts, the prognosis is not good. A disappointed heart will eventually become a darkened heart. It can become cynical, idealistic, and have difficulty seeing the good in anything around it. We all know people (maybe you're one of them) who used to love coming to church, worshipping, and being with the saints. Suddenly, they are nowhere to be found. Disappointment caused their spiritual eyesight to become impaired, and they lost the ability to see the good in the church. This is why praise, prayer, worship, and staying connected to the church are vital to the health and life of every believer, disappointed or not.

Remember, "... *it is God who works in you, both to will and to do for His good pleasure*" (Philippians 2:13, ESV). Overcome the giant of disappointment by knowing God is doing something good for you. You don't have to rebel. You never have to pick up a stone, and you don't have to allow disappointment to rule in your life. Be a person after God's own heart and watch what He will do in every situation!

7

WHEN AN IDEAL IS NOT SO IDEAL!

What is an ideal? It is a person's ultimate perception of what something should be. We have ideals about religion, education, friendship, love, health, eating, and so on. Our lives are full of ideals. We all have our own ideas about the way things should be and what life's perfect scenario is. For right or for wrong, these ideals are what shape our thinking, attitude, and actions.

Before we go any further, let me clarify the context from which I am confronting idealism. I am not saying all ideals are wrong or bad. Throughout history, many great accomplishments have resulted from individuals standing for what they believed to be right. There is a time to hold fast to one's ideals and a time to let them go. The trick comes in knowing when to do so. For example, if you were about to be martyred for your faith in God, that is not the time to give up your ideals. There are situations that do call for us to stand with unwavering loyalty for what we believe in. Clearly, I don't mean those times. I am talking about the occasions that seem so significant to us in the moment, but in the grand scheme of things are very insignificant.

In this chapter, I want to examine why misappropriated ideals can lead to rebellion in a person's life. I'm concerned with the strife and division caused in the body of Christ by idealistic people, who insist upon majoring on minor issues related to their own mindsets. Nowhere is this more prevalent than in the church, where everyone seems to have an opinion of how it should look and act.

I appeal to you, brothers, by the name of our Lord Jesus Christ,
that all of you agree, and that there be no divisions among you,
but that you be united in the same mind and the same judgment.
                                                   —1 CORINTHIANS 1:10, ESV

There are people who are departing from the churches they once loved and were a part of just because of something that runs contrary to their ideals. Many of them are exceptional, sincere people; however, their insistence on maintaining their ideals causes disunity and dysfunction in the body of Christ. Many people use their viewpoints as a means to escape the lack of perfection they find in the church, but these perspectives don't count for a hill of beans with God, regardless of how relevant or right they may be. If it begins to affect our lives in an unhealthy manner, and we obsess to the point where all life is viewed through that lens, then it is no longer idyllic. It's all right to have ideals, but if they begin to bear bad fruit, maybe we need to examine why.

Here's an example I'm sure we've all encountered in church. God powerfully touches a person in revival; they testify of their transformation and everything looks good. Later on, someone notices a discrepancy in that person's behaviour and thinks, *If they were so revived, how could they still act inappropriately? If they were really touched by God, they wouldn't act like that!* In their minds, revival means perfection, and if someone around them falls short, they easily become disillusioned, because their ideals are challenged.

Idealism says, "If they truly loved me, they would never hurt me." How often has a person walked away from church because of a perceived lack of love? After all, if anyone is able to walk in love, it should certainly be the church-goers. When I was a student in Bible College, there was a particular teacher that I loved and admired. I remember seeing him in the foyer after church. I wanted to share something that the Lord had done for me. He was in the middle of a conversation, so I waited anxiously for them to finish. I could hardly wait to tell him the good news. As soon as they were done, I quickly began my story, but he interrupted me saying, "Not right now, I am busy!" And away he went.

As a new believer, I hadn't experienced any kind of rejection from Christians, and it was new to me. To be honest, I didn't think such a thing was even possible. Of course, I was naive and ultra-spiritual, and it hurt. I stood there in shock, feeling rejected, and then walked out of the church in anger. I was familiar with rejection before I became a believer, but I never expected it to happen in the church.

Driving home from church that day, all sorts of movies played in my mind. You know, little scenarios of me straightening him out, speaking my mind, and making sure he knew what he did to me. Of course, all of these thoughts were justified through my own self-righteousness. As I continued to dwell on my so-called injustice, more voices told me there was no love in this church, and if they were true believers, then this wouldn't have happened.

I drove on, and the Lord began challenging my idealistic image of how church people should act. It was like He said, "Brent, it's not what happens to you, but how you respond to it that matters. Will you walk away rejected and angry, or will you forgive and continue to walk in love?" Well, I learned a hard but wonderful lesson, which still benefits me to this day. A believer may see what is less than ideal as their justification to separate from the body of Christ, but that doesn't hold water.

IT'S AN INSIDE JOB

The church is being attacked from without and within. It is one thing to be attacked from the outside, but when the greatest threat is coming from the inside, something must be done! The enemy is doing his very best to destroy the foundations of the church, because it is the greatest threat to his aspirations on the earth. If he can get the church to struggle with its identity and purpose, he can then destroy its very foundations, which were built on the apostles and prophets, with Jesus being the cornerstone.

I believe the enemy of our souls is desperate and is doing his very best to cause division within the church. He knows the best way to do this is to work from the inside out. All he has to do is get the church people to criticize one another, and he wins. It's an inside job! He is sowing seeds of strife that ultimately cause division as people fail to understand that unity is more important to God than perfect church structure or doctrine. When someone falls into this trap, they begin to allow a divisive spirit to operate in their lives, and the enemy snickers as they fall prey to his insidious schemes.

Now it's not like this has never happened before, but it seems to have accelerated in the last ten years or so. Never before have so many people questioned the church, its foundations, or its identity. One only needs to look on the Internet, in bookstores, or on Facebook to see or hear the confusion floating around regarding the church. Because of this, many have walked away, believing that their true purpose and fulfillment can only be found outside the church. This is a lie, and if this seed is left to grow, it will become a huge deception and cause many to stumble. We cannot allow this to happen! All the enemy needs to do is shed some doubt about our ideals and we struggle. Here is a small list of the seeds of destruction being felt among people today:

- *I got hurt in church.*
- *The church is holding me back from ministry, or my calling.*
- *We must go out to the streets, instead of being stuck inside these four walls (Good one, but not worth abandoning the church over!).*
- *The church's foundations are wrong, so we must rethink the whole thing.*
- *It is not organic enough.*
- *Too much man-in-control.*
- *They made us sit where we didn't want to (Wow!).*
- *I wanted to prophesy, dance, and wave flags whenever I felt led, but they didn't let me.*
- *The leaders weren't perfect, so how could I follow them.*
- *I'm just not good with people.*
- *I have no friends there.*
- *Too many rules to follow.*

• *I tithed, but never saw the return I was expecting.*

• *I thought I would be happier.*

These are just a few of the reasons people have given, over the years, to justify their departure to "greener pastures." They all seem to have one thing in common—they are unhappy and blame the church for it. The result is broken relationships, confusion, lack of unity, and ultimately, a church void of the power and presence of God. When people leave the church, there is a vacuum left in their wake, and the church is not better for it, but worse. Just because a person gets hurt, disappointed or discouraged in the church, should he now throw the whole thing out? Do we throw out the baby with the bathwater, or do we just clean up the baby?

UNFULFILLED IDEALS

Couples often approach marriage with many preconceived ideals in place. The woman wants a knight in shining armour to sweep her off her feet and whisk her away into the sunset. The man wants someone like his mother, who will always forgive him, do everything for him, and make it all better. It sounds wonderful until you get hurt by the very one who was supposed to love you the most. I mean, how could someone who loves me hurt me so much? This idealism can be very painful because reality, for the most part, doesn't live up to the fantasies in our heads, and until we realize that, we will continually struggle to be happy.

UNFULFILLED IDEALISM ABOUT CHURCH LEADS TO CONFUSION, FRUSTRATION, AND DISAPPOINTMENT BECAUSE WE AREN'T GETTING WHAT WE THINK GOD PROMISED US.

Much of the rebellion against the church has come from a mindset that is idealistic in nature. We have high expectations for leaders, churches, and ministries, and too many people become shipwrecked when their ideals are not met. We become disillusioned by our idealism. Unfulfilled idealism about church leads to confusion, frustration, and discouragement because we aren't getting what we think God promised us.

As we read the Bible, we can easily become a people who are looking for the idealistic church, one that is perfect and without fault or trouble. The problem is that this viewpoint is askew from what is real. If things don't happen exactly as we have read in the Bible, we can become discouraged and suspicious, thinking it has to be just so, or it can't be of God. This is a deception. It will lead people to become rebellious, and get caught up in what is ideal, to the exclusion of what is real. Their desire for the ideal blinds them to the greatness of what already exists. This, in turn, causes them to devalue and abandon what they already possess. The result is people become rebellious toward the church, its structure, and its leaders. I want to make one thing perfectly clear—most of those who rebel against the church are not evil people, but they have convinced themselves they are right, and that even God is on their side! They think they are correct, and the whole church world is wrong.

GOD IS NEVER ON THE SIDE OF THE REBELLIOUS!

Listen friend, even if you *think* you're right as you speak out against established authority, you will end up being wrong! God is never on the side of the rebellious! He is not the author of rebellion!

MY STRUGGLE

As a pastor, I have struggled with my idealistic mindset concerning the church and revival. I have longed for, prayed, and believed for revival for many years, and have a passion to see God move powerfully in the church. Although we have seen many wonderful and powerful moves of the Holy Spirit, I know there is so much more to see and experience. When I don't see everything I want to, I can become discouraged. Like many pastors, I have quit on Sunday afternoon, only to hire myself back on Monday (Ha-ha)! If I allow these ideals to lead and guide me, they can actually do more harm than good. This is why we must always take a good, long look at what we have, not at what we don't have.

Often people have come to our church and waxed eloquent about how great it was. Of course, I appreciate what they are saying, but I must be on guard not to grow familiar with the good things around me and take them for granted. I am thankful for the people God has brought around me, who can see the forest for the trees, and continue to keep me on the straight and narrow road of optimism.

Being idealistic is not so ideal when it saps our strength and vision, or tempts us to give up or quit. We must be careful not to allow our ideals to become hindrances to the completion of what God has called us to do. I am called to be a pastor, and I must be faithful to it no matter what is happening with the state of revival in my church. When we desire something so strongly, it is easy to blame people when it doesn't happen in accordance with our idealistic mindset.

MINISTRY LEADERSHIP CAN BE DERAILED WHEN IDEALISM AND REALITY FAIL TO MERGE.

Ministry leadership can be derailed when idealism and reality fail to merge. Misplaced ideals can rob us of the joy of being a leader in the church. Hope deferred is a huge source of discouragement in the ministry; therefore, we must purpose to continue on with what God called us to do, regardless of our unfulfilled expectations. Our joy must not come from what we see or don't see; it must come from our relationship with the Lord. While we should not stop desiring and believing for the ideal (it's okay to want the ideal), we cannot allow our unfulfilled expectations to destroy our faith, hope, and love.

Many people, being discouraged by their ideals, can lose the joy of what is before them or what they already possess. Some grow weary of church services, measuring them by the early miracles, signs, and wonders they read about in the book of Acts. They begin to "dis" the church, complaining about its "lack thereof," but squawking about it "won't change a thing." It is one thing to talk about what the church should or shouldn't do; it's quite another to actively be part of the solution. Many leave church disgruntled by the failure of the ideal, but leaving is not the answer. It's time to stop walking away! We must not allow unfulfilled expectations to dictate our response.

People tend to think idyllically in many areas of life. People who have an ideal vision of marriage will certainly become discouraged if it doesn't meet their expectations. Many divorces result from an idealistic mindset regarding marriage. People become unhappy when their current situation doesn't line up with what they have envisioned.

We can read the Bible and see the ideal, but what do we do when our lives don't line up? Will we become discouraged, give up, or rebel against it because we don't see it? Many people have given up on church because the expectations they had weren't met. How many times have we become critical of something or someone for the same reasons?

I can't tell you how many times I have allowed my ideals about God, church, or believers to cloud my thinking and cause me to become half-hearted in pastoring. I have come to the conclusion that, regardless of whatever unfulfilled ideals I have, I cannot let them deter me from my calling, or from my commitment and faithfulness to God and to His church.

How many times has a pastor or leader used the pulpit to voice his idealistic desires? They would rather preach their ideals than say something to help the people. I can honestly say I have been guilty of this, but for the most part I am learning to let go and not grow discouraged when things don't happen according to my timetable. This is an important principle for all leaders to learn.

In my youthful days, when we wanted to communicate, we just picked up the stationary handset and rotary dialed the number. Modern computers were housed in a large building, and no one dreamed that one day you could hold one in the palm of your hand. We have all benefited from the increase in technology. The World Wide Web has provided a whole new pulpit from which anyone's ideals can be proclaimed. As wonderful as this is, we must exercise caution about what we preach on social media, as it can affect a multitude of people. The Internet is flooded with people who are struggling with unfulfilled ideals, declaring all kinds of mixed up opinions, ideas, and doctrines. Here's some that are prevalent:

- Universal salvation (everyone will be saved regardless of personal belief).
- Hyper grace (taking the grace message to extremes).
- Tithing is not for today.
- The Old Testament is meaningless.
- Don't read the red letters (Paul's revelations are more important than Jesus').
- There is no judgment or hell.
- Leaders are no longer required.
- No more works of the ministry (apparently all we need to do is rest).

I believe many of these deviations from sound doctrine are a direct result of unfulfilled ideals.

Idealistic Leadership — is There Such a Thing?

Many people have an ideal about leadership in the church, and when it is disrupted, they become discouraged and struggle to continue following. If their opinion of a leader is shattered, then they no longer feel they can follow him/her. We must remember we are all flawed in some fashion. Leaders aren't perfect, and they will never live up to our idealistic fantasies. The same goes for the leader who is scrutinizing the people. He, too, has an idealistic viewpoint about what people should be like. He can easily fall prey to the same temptation and begin to look at church people with a critical attitude, thinking, *If only they would be more committed, give more, and listen better, we would have a great revival or see all we want to see.* It is true that if people were more committed, everyone would benefit; however, leaders must not let their ideals hinder their love for the people.

Majoring on Minors

We think God cares about doctrines and rules as much as we do, but He is most interested in unity. People surmise that what they believe is more important than unity, but is it? God allowed David to have several wives, even though the law said the King was to have only one. God overlooked this because He saw what was in David's heart. A mistake made out of a good heart can still turn out okay, but one made from a bad heart may not end well.

CORRECT CHURCH OPERATION IS LESS IMPORTANT THAN HAVING ONE HEART AND ONE MIND.

God will, at times, overlook imperfection to find unity. Correct church operation is less important than having one heart and one mind. So many churches have divided because of people who were in disagreement over doctrine, vision, or structure. What an indictment against the church!

Many feel it is their God-given duty to expose the less than ideal church they see, and they do it at the expense of unity. What they don't realize is that when you attack the body, you are actually attacking yourself. That's why this is encouraged by the devil. One of his favourite tactics is to cause friendly-fire among Christians. It makes him smile when he can sit back and watch us bite and devour each other over disputes such as:

- *Holy Spirit or Holy Ghost? He's the same.*
- *Water Baptism: in the name of the Father, Son, and Holy Ghost (What if we forget one of them, oh no?).*
- *Demons: possessed or oppressed (Who cares, just get rid of them, I say!).*
- *King James only! After all, this is the version Jesus read (Ha-ha, He read Aramaic or Hebrew).*
- *Old Testament vs. New Testament (It's all God's Word).*
- *Pre, mid, post or no tribulation (Just be ready!).*
- *Casual vs. formal wear in church (To each his own).*
- *Grace vs. works (You can't have one without the other!).*

- *The book of Acts church ("A must in order to see God move!" NO, not really!).*

For you were called to be free, brothers; only don't use this freedom as an opportunity for the flesh, but serve one another through love. For the entire law is fulfilled in one statement: Love your neighbor as yourself. But if you bite and devour one another, watch out, or you will be consumed by one another. —GALATIANS 5:13–15

Paul's message to the Galatians was given to help restore peace between first century Jews and Gentiles, who, for the first time in many years, were serving the same God. If the devil can get in and cause us to criticize one another, he wins;, regardless of what we're fighting over. We can think we have won the battle, only to lose the war. We don't want to lose the battle for unity by majoring on minors. When we hold too tightly to our ideals, we run the risk of causing disunity, which weakens the strength and power of God in the church. Are we willing to sacrifice the presence of God on the altar of our own opinions?

WE CANNOT BECOME REBELLIOUS BECAUSE OF
MISPLACED OR MISUNDERSTOOD IDEALS.
FAITH BUILT ON REBELLION WILL ULTIMATELY FAIL!

God isn't necessarily trying to change the system so much as He wants to change our hearts. The church always was and always will be His vehicle. If our hearts get messed up, it's over! We cannot become rebellious because of misplaced or misunderstood ideals. Faith built on rebellion will ultimately fail!

IS GOD THE ULTIMATE IDEALIST?

You know; God isn't as idealistic as we think He is! Think about it. As an idealist, would God have created man, knowing all along what his capacity for evil was? He knew exactly what would happen, yet He still made mankind. Is that the mindset of an idealist? If He was the perfect idealist, He would have built into Adam the ability to automatically overcome any and all temptations. Being omniscient, He created man with a will of his own, and the ability to make his own decisions, regardless of the outcome.

It's possible for people to believe that God is the ultimate idealist. In their efforts to emulate what they think He is, they become idealistic themselves and go to extremes, thinking they are going to bat for the Lord. Anything taken to the extreme has the potential to destroy, and if we aren't careful, our ideals can drive us to destruction.

How many religious groups or cults have sprung up, all believing they are the only ones who are truly in God's will? Too many well-meaning, goodhearted people end up being destroyed by the very ideals for which they have lived. People have spent enormous amounts of time, effort, and money trying to bring their ideals into reality, only to see them go up in smoke.

A TIME FOR EVERYTHING

> For everything there is a season, a time for every activity under heaven. A time to be born and a time to die. A time to plant and a time to harvest. A time to kill and a time to heal. A time to tear down and a time to build up. A time to cry and a time to laugh. A time to grieve and a time to dance. A time to scatter stones and a time to gather stones. A time to embrace and a time to turn away. A time to search and a time to quit searching. A time to keep and a time to throw away. A time to tear and a time to mend. A time to be quiet and a time to speak. A time to love and a time to hate, a time for war and a time for peace.
>
> —ECCLESIASTES 3:1–8, NLT

King Solomon, the wisest man who ever lived, explained a little of what life is all about. In his wisdom, he said, "There is a time for everything under the sun." Solomon summed up all of life's endeavours in total contrast to each other, but they give beautiful balance to life. For instance, it doesn't say there is only a time to cry, but also a time to laugh. Both are normal and right. God created us to live a life of balance, not too far off one way or another. We could add that there is a time to pursue the ideal, and a time to be content in imperfection.

Let me say this again—there is a time to be idealistic. Some might say it takes an idealist to follow Jesus, and they might be correct. Obviously, it takes an idealist to die to oneself and live a sacrificial life for the Lord. It is always right to stand for your ideals when they involve faithfulness and loyalty to Jesus.

BALANCE, THE IDEALISM KILLER!

IDEALISTS CAN END UP SO CONSUMED BY THEIR BELIEFS
THAT THEY BECOME UNHEALTHY AND DANGEROUS TO
THEMSELVES AND THE PEOPLE THEY ARE CONNECTED TO.

Without balance, we are prone to let our ideals take us off course. Idealists can end up so consumed by their beliefs that they become unhealthy and dangerous to themselves and the people they are connected to. Bringing balance in is the only way to be free from idealism: *"A false balance is an abomination to the Lord, but a just weight is his delight"* (Proverbs 11:1, KJV); *"A just balance and scales are the Lord's; all the weights in the bag are his work"* (Proverbs 16:11, ESV).

There are times in life when we may be extreme or idealistic about something, but we must always remember to come back into balance. Right now, juicing has become the craze in our church. Everyone is buying a machine, and organic vegetables are being sacrificed for the greater good. The ideal is that juicing gives them plenty of vitamins and minerals for proper health. So what do people do? They go on an all-out juicing binge. The problem arises when people decide more is better, so they drink twenty glasses of juice per day. I once had a friend who juiced so many carrots that his skin turned orange, and he felt terrible. The doctor ran tests and told him to cut out the juice because it was adversely affecting his health. Was the problem the juice itself? Is it wrong to want to be healthy? No, the problem wasn't the juice, but an unbalanced approach to it. What started out as ideal soon became detrimental.

What I learned in grade two was that a balanced diet, exercise, and plenty of rest are still the best ways to maintain good health. We need to learn that sometimes too much of a good thing is just not good! I like chocolate (a lot), but too much of it will have an unfavourable effect on my health.

WE MUST NEVER ALLOW OUR IDEALS TO OVERRIDE COMMON SENSE.

Common sense dictates that too much of almost anything is not good. My finding is that common sense is rather uncommon. We must never allow our ideals to override common sense.

Without advocating lazy and apathetic Christianity, I need to say something about spiritual life. Prayer is important, but should we pray 24/7 and do nothing else? No, of course not! Should we read the Word of God day and night, to the exclusion of natural life? No, we cannot. There is a life to be lived out in the spiritual and in the natural; both are essential and valid. The problem occurs when we go to extremes with one or the other.

I am a preacher who speaks constantly about being on fire for God and having a passion for Jesus. Our church regularly has corporate prayer meetings, and we are all looking to be in His manifest presence, but there are many things we need to do in the natural as well if we are to fulfill the Lord's commission to make disciples of all nations. Much of this requires us to live and work in the natural. I like this statement that Charles Finney often quoted from St. Augustine: "Pray like it all depends on God, but work like it all depends on you!"[10]

Let me show you another example where balance is needed. We have all seen the guy who has a muscular upper torso, but his legs are spindly and out of proportion. What we have here is an out of balance approach to looking good. I always laugh to myself when I see it. You can have the largest arms in the world, but if your legs are tiny, or your core is weak, you will be limited in how much weight you can lift.

This is why many idealists become unstable. They overemphasize one area to the exclusion of another and become unbalanced in their

WHEN AN IDEAL IS NOT SO IDEAL!

approach to life. I'm sure we have all experienced this from time to time, but we must always be aware of what is going on in and around us. I have found that most of us are not good judges of our own lives, so it is beneficial to have people around who will tell us the truth. Iron sharpens iron!

Jesus, the Balanced Idealist

He said to them, "Come away by yourselves to a remote place and rest for a while." For many people were coming and going, and they did not even have time to eat. –MARK 6:31

We can name people from years past who were idealistic in their approach to ministry and gave their whole lives to it. They believed the anointing made them invincible, no matter how they lived or how hard they pushed their bodies. Their early deaths are an example for us to learn from. Their ideal of ministry was to go as hard as possible and never take a break. After all, people were dying and going to hell. While this is certainly true, no one can go and go forever without proper rest. Think about this— Jesus only had about three years to get His purpose accomplished, but He still took the time to rest. Jesus knew the value of balance when it came to life and ministry. I'm sure He had a better understanding of the struggles going on in the world, both spiritually and physically, but He still took the time to recharge. If He had to, how much more do we?

A person could read this and think I'm saying that people who work hard in ministry are idealists out of touch with reality. I would never advocate that. All believers should give their whole life to the advancement of God's Kingdom on the earth. When it's time to work … work, and when it's time to rest … rest! A balanced approach will keep us from falling prey to the ideals that drive us.

For the love of money is a root of all kinds of evils. It is through this craving that some have wandered away from the faith and pierced themselves with many pangs. –1 TIMOTHY 6:10, ESV

The idea that money can fix all of our problems, or give us the happiness we desire, has been a major source of trouble. Many marriages have broken up because of a love of money. While money is necessary and valuable to give us a higher quality of life, it must be used with knowledge and wisdom. I am using money to make a point because it is normal and right to want money. The problem comes when we spend more time and energy than is proper for the acquiring of it. Almost any ideal, even one that is right and normal, if taken to extreme, has the potential to cause trouble in our lives.

UNBALANCED IDEALISM PROMISES US
MORE THAN IT CAN DELIVER, AND
COSTS US MORE THAN WE CAN PAY!

There are too many ideals to list in this chapter, but they all have the inherent power to deceive if we fail to understand this concept. The deception that comes with pursuing our ideals, regardless of the cost, is that if we do manage to catch them, untold happiness will be ours. It's just like the pot of gold promised at the end of a rainbow. Unbalanced idealism promises us more than it can deliver, and costs us more than we can pay!

SELF-RIGHTEOUS EXCLUSIVENESS

At the beginning of this chapter, I wrote about the importance of unity. I've seen people become exclusive because they believe their ideals are more important than staying in touch with the greater body of Christ. Their strong viewpoints lead them to withdraw from the local church because they think no one understands them, or they can no longer receive anything there. This idealistic self-righteousness is not of God. God never uses self-righteousness to justify exclusivity.

Some depart from the church because they think that by staying they are endorsing what they perceive to be wrong. Most of these grievances are minor and not worthy of such an extreme response. God is more concerned with overall unity than nit-picking at minor issues.

As we close this chapter, we need to ask ourselves if any of our ideals are motivating rebellion against the church. Have we allowed our opinions of how things should be to cause us to back off from the place where God has called us? Has our idealism caused us to become suspicious or critical of the institution we once loved and held dear to our hearts?

We all have a set of ideals that we live our lives by, and they influence us for either right or wrong. Maybe, even in a small way, they have created an imbalance in our lives. Some ideals are worth fighting for, and some aren't. We need to make sure we are picking the right fight! When an ideal sparks disunity or division in the church, then perhaps it's time to re-examine our motives.

WE ALL NEED TO TAKE REGULAR INVENTORY OF
OUR IDEALS TO SEE IF THEY'VE BECOME MISPLACED
AND ARE CAUSING IMBALANCE IN OUR LIVES.

Take a look at your life at this moment. Have your ideals taken you too far one way or another in any area? Perhaps they have put a strain on your marriage or your relationships at work. Are you pulling away from church and fellowship with other believers? We all need to take regular inventory of our ideals to see if they've become misplaced and are causing an imbalance in our lives.

I encourage you to think about what I've said and allow the Holy Spirit to reveal any ideals that might be frustrating you and causing you to back away from the body of Christ. In the big picture, are those ideals more important than the advancement of God's Kingdom on the earth? God's ideal is the church, and He will never stray from that, so let those frustrations go, brush yourself off, take up your cross, and follow Jesus!

8.

You're So
RELIGIOUS!

But know this: Difficult times will come in the last days. For people will be lovers of self, lovers of money, boastful, proud, blasphemers, disobedient to parents, ungrateful, unholy, unloving, irreconcilable, slanderers without self-control, brutal, without love for what is good, traitors, reckless, conceited lovers of pleasure rather than lovers of God, holding to the form of godliness but denying its power. Avoid these people! —2 TIMOTHY 3:1–5

You're so religious! How many times have I heard this expression? Indeed, I have often used it myself. I used to think I understood what it meant as I applied it wherever it seemed to fit. Since then, I have come to question the true meaning of the term "religious." What does it really mean?

Many years ago, we had a man minister at our church who had been mightily impacted under the ministry of Rodney Howard-Browne, who was known for powerful manifestations of the Holy Ghost, one of which was termed "holy laughter." The guest minister would play and sing songs about the new wine of the Holy Spirit, preach, and then pray for people to be filled with the Holy Ghost and experience laughter. Night after night, the music, preaching, and ministry would be of this nature, and many people were powerfully touched. It was wonderful to see! However, at every meeting, there seemed to be an underlying feeling, or implied belief, that anyone who didn't manifest holy laughter was "religious."

At the time, I was the Young Adults pastor. Most of the younger crowd loved to lie on the floor, laugh, and flow in that particular manifestation of God. When I saw this wasn't happening to someone, I would think, *They are so religious!* or *They need to be set free from their religion so they can operate in the same freedom that us "nonreligious" folks are experiencing.*

After a few weeks, our pastor felt we should bring in some other people to preach and minister so that the move of God would be more balanced and not so one-dimensional. When we told the guest minister about this, he immediately disagreed; he felt this was the move of God at the time, and anything else was religious. Our pastor tried to reason with him, but to no avail. Either it was Holy Ghost, new-wine songs and laughter, or he was gone. Well, I don't have to tell you what happened, do I? I learned a valuable lesson through this, and began to question what being religious truly entailed.

You might ask, "What's the big deal?" It's this: idealistic viewpoints about what being religious is, or is not, became a contentious issue that stopped what God wanted to do within the church. Instead of flowing with our leadership, the minister took his proverbial bat and ball and went home. Idealistic beliefs about religion have prompted many people to rebel against sound leadership.

Not too long ago, when people were dancing in one of our services, someone nudged me saying, "Dance!" Come to think of it, this has happened a few times over the years. The look on their face said that if I didn't dance at that very moment, I was being religious. Was I missing it? It's not as if I couldn't or wouldn't dance. I have been known to kick up my heels a time or two. It bugged me that I was being labeled "religious" because I didn't dance at that moment. Now, I agree that sometimes we do need a little encouragement to get out of our fleshly, carnal nature and experience the joy and freedom that comes from dancing before the Lord, but the situation taught me something.

WE OFTEN LABEL ANYONE WHO DOES NOT MOVE EXACTLY
THE WAY WE WANT THEM TO AS "RELIGIOUS."

When people don't move exactly the way we want them to, we often label them "religious." I understand that the church needs to be more responsive to the Lord but at what point are we acting religiously? I'm not trying to be the "religious police," but we must not allow our idea of "being religious," to cause us to rebel against the church or its leadership. Perhaps it's time to study this term and try to make more sense out of it.

Re-Defining Religious

Our church meets together three times a week—once for corporate prayer and twice for services. Believe it or not, people have commented about us, saying we are religious because we go to church so much. Does going to a building to pray, worship, listen to a preacher, and receive prayer, constitute being religious? If so, does staying away from church make us nonreligious?

In the current climate of pro-church vs. anti-church believers, this issue must be addressed. Too many believers have come to the false conclusion that church activities are religious and must be shunned. How untrue!

Before we go on, let's seek to understand why people seem to be so terrified of being religious. Why did we adopt this term in the first place? For what reasons are we so afraid of being labeled as religious? I believe we adopted the term because we think all religion (religious ideas, beliefs, etc.) has the ability to hinder God; therefore, we must seek to escape its devilish grasp. I can agree with that to a point, but we have misused and misapplied the term and created improper fears in the Body of Christ, to the detriment of God's Word.

> ... *traitors, reckless, conceited lovers of pleasure rather than lovers of God, holding to the form of godliness but denying its power. Avoid these people!* –2 TIMOTHY 3:4–5

These verses give us some insight on this topic. The ESV says, "... *having the appearance of godliness, but denying its power. Avoid such people*" (2 Timothy 3:5). What is the problem here? Is it having the appearance of godliness, or is it denying godliness's power? Most of the accusations about being religious revolve around outward appearances, and not on whether or not God's power is evident. I believe we have falsely equated one with the other. In singular terms, looking religious indicates a lack of power. Is this true? If I look religious to someone, am I void of the presence and power of God? Can appearances alone hinder, God?

RELIGIOUS TIES??

Do you think the Holy Spirit would be released to move more powerfully among us if we got rid of our dress clothes in favour of more casual attire? Is God threatened by our nice clothes? If we dress in a casual manner—t-shirt, shorts, sandals—and drink a latte, will it cause God's presence and power to increase in our lives?

Sometimes I wear a tie. In fact, I enjoy it. One day a fellow minister came up to me and told me he got delivered from ties (religion). Seriously? He was delivered from the evil, religious, and God-hindering tie! Wow! Those ties must possess horrible evil! It's hilarious when we step back and look at it, isn't it? The perception of being religious is often closely tied to appearance, dress code, and the like.

I've often wondered how many people want to dress like the hippies of the sixties and seventies, thinking those guys looked more like Jesus than anyone else. While the Bible does stress the importance of dressing modestly, it doesn't say anything in relation to clothing being religious (form of godliness, but denying the power). We must conclude that we may all have different tastes concerning the clothes we wear, but it does not determine if we are religious.

CONCERNING SPONTANEITY

There is also a misunderstanding about spiritual activity. Some believers think all spiritual activity should be done spontaneously, believing the Holy Spirit will be more involved that way.

Is God unable to speak or direct, except spontaneously?

I have heard many preachers say, "I had something all ready to preach, but just before I got up here, the Lord gave me something else." Now, while this can occasionally happen, it still begs the question: wasn't God speaking to you while you were preparing to preach? Was your preparation all in vain? Is God unable to speak or direct, except spontaneously? When He does speak at the last minute, does it result in a more powerful presence and move of God? Is God only present in the spontaneous times?

I know ministers who refuse to prepare beforehand, saying they don't want to quench the Spirit of God. I have heard some of these so-called "I preach by the spirit" ministers, and I have to say, they aren't any more powerful or anointed than the prepared guys! Furthermore, the prepared guys tended to have more meat and potatoes in their sermons than the "fly by the seat of your pants" preachers.

A number of years ago, a guest minister spoke at our church, and he loved to proclaim how he never prepared a sermon and only preached by the Spirit of God. After one of the services, he was going on about this, and our pastor replied, "Yes, we can tell!" I don't think the guy was too impressed with that, but it was the truth!

While we all should be open to the move of the Holy Ghost at any given time, we should also be prepared beforehand. Unfortunately, too many have eliminated one in favour of the other. We should be open to both. Our example should be the early Apostles, who spent much time in the Word of God and prayer. Time spent in advance with God, in study and prayer, can open the door for powerful moments of spontaneity. Unfortunately, we have equated true spirituality with the spontaneous. The problem with this thinking is that it creates an "off the wall" mentality that says preparation is not of God and labels it as religious. Again, not true! Being spontaneous is the *exception*, not the rule!

Structure Versus no Structure

Is God able to move more freely in a structured or unstructured church service? Is there a right answer? I don't know if there is, but I know I've seen God move in both. Some believe having a format will hinder the spontaneity of the Holy Spirit. They say, "I am only led by the Spirit. I only pray and worship when God tells me to do so!" Either way, the problem occurs when we don't allow room for the Holy Spirit to move. The way we do church is not the problem; leaving no room for the Holy Spirit is the problem!

TRUE LIFE AND POWER DO NOT COME FROM SERVICE
STRUCTURE, BUT RATHER, FROM THE
HEARTS AND LIVES OF THE BELIEVERS WITHIN IT.

There are whole churches and groups who are working frantically to try to change the entire structure of their services in the hope that it will produce more life and greater results. While this could be a good thing to do, it doesn't guarantee anything. True life and power do not come from service structure, but from the hearts and lives of the believers within it. If the people lack a hunger and thirst for God, are apathetic to the Word, or simply don't care, then regardless of the structure used, it will not produce life. The problem is not the structure, but the spiritual health of the people *within* the structure.

While it is great to be led by the Spirit, we must be careful not to conclude that specific structures or religion always hinder God. He doesn't have the hang-ups we have. He can move in any situation if given half a chance. We shouldn't write off any denomination, group, or church because we disagree with their structure. A lack of structure can inhibit the moving of the Holy Ghost, just as much as having it can. Again, the trend is to be extreme, moving from one end of the spectrum to the other. As I have said time and time again, balance is critical.

In our church, we have put some safeguards in place as a protective measure for the wonderful and faithful people who attend. We want to keep them safe from people who slip in the back and, of their own accord, randomly pray and prophesy over them. Our ushers are trained to spot this and stop it immediately. Sometimes the correction is received; other times, those visitors storm out very angry and upset, saying we are religious and are hindering the movement of the Holy Ghost. The truth of the matter is that they had no authority to come into another assembly and speak. They were interfering with our structure by trying to impose theirs. This isn't spiritual freedom, but spiritual rebellion. If they truly believed God had something to say to someone, they would have contacted the leaders and asked permission to share it. We have no problem allowing the Holy Ghost to move, but we have a God-given responsibility to protect those He has placed in our spiritual care. People who overstep this principle are not walking in spiritual power or freedom, but in rebellion. God is not the author of so-called spirit led rebellion.

By the way, God is not in favour of back room or parking lot prophets. All prophecy needs to be done with at least some measure of leadership present to protect and judge what is being said. There are just too many wolves walking around masquerading as good sheep. I hope believers won't disregard proper safety measures in their desire to hear a Word from the Lord!

SPIRITUAL FREE-FOR-ALL

But everything must be done decently and in order.
                              —1 CORINTHIANS 14:40

Some people believe that the end time move of God will be a time when structure and authority are reduced to a spiritual free-for-all where anything goes. While this sounds fantastic to many, I don't buy into it at all. I've been in meetings where this was done, and it ended up being chaotic. Everyone had a prophetic word, a teaching, a song, or a "this is what I feel God wants us to do" attitude. While it may make everyone feel important when they get up to do their thing, we must remember that God doesn't have multiple personality disorder. He isn't going to have twenty different directions and movements happening at the same time. It is not an "every man does what is right in his own heart" kind of thing.

This does not mean we disallow people from operating in their various gifts; it just means that a little structure could go a long way in seeing a powerful move of God in our midst. God wants to move, and it is our task to make sure He is given every freedom to do so, but not at the expense of Biblical principles and the order given in the Word of God. While it is extremely important for all of us to be led by the Spirit of God, we must also see how vital it is to do things decently, in order, and in total submission to the local spiritual authorities.

OUT OF THE BOX

Some believers think that attending church on a regular basis for prayer, worship, and the Word is being religious. They always come up with things like, "God isn't in a box and He wants you to get out of yours!" What they are saying is that operating via structure puts them and God into a box. They think it must be avoided at all cost. Is this true? If we have set times for meeting with God, is He somehow hindered from moving in our lives? Let's look at Jesus, Paul, and the disciples and try to understand this more clearly.

JESUS:

"*He came to Nazareth, where He had been brought up. As usual, He entered the synagogue on the Sabbath day and stood up to read*" (Luke 4:16). Notice it says, "*as usual.*" The KJV says, "As his custom was." In other words, this was His habit. Jesus went to the synagogue to be part of the group on a weekly, or perhaps, daily basis. Jesus had set times for being in the synagogue. Mark 10:1 says, "*...as He usually did, He began teaching them once more.*" Jesus taught the people regularly, as was His custom. I think many believers today have misunderstood Jesus in first century context. For the last six hundred years, the Protestant movement has led us to believe in a whitewashed, European descended, English-speaking Christ, but the truth is that *Jesus was a Jew.* He dressed, looked, and acted like a Jew. He was probably even a Pharisee (yes, tassels and phylacteries included). He lived out and obeyed all of the Torah, and likely included some of the traditions of His day. Jesus attended the synagogue on a regular basis as was expected of devout Jews. He even participated in the traditional reading of the Torah. When some of them did not like His teachings, they couldn't throw Him out, because He *obeyed* the rules.

Paul:

What about Paul? Obviously, he changed everything. Or did he? Acts 17:2 says, *"As usual, Paul went to the synagogue, and on three Sabbath days reasoned with them from the Scriptures…"* Again, it says *"as usual"* or, *"as was his custom."* Paul, too, had pre-set times to be in the synagogue. He also kept the Torah, participated in all the feasts at their appointed times, and obeyed all the laws handed down by the Jewish fathers and leaders. The Jews knew the power in set times and still know it today. Why do the Gentiles struggle so much with it?

Early Disciples:

How about these guys? Surely they were led by *spiritual freedom* all the time. Yet the Bible says, *"Every day they devoted themselves to meeting together in the temple complex …"* (Acts 2:46), and *"Now Peter and John were going up together to the temple complex at the hour of prayer at three in the afternoon"* (Acts 3:1). Scripture says they went specifically at the third hour to pray, worship, and study the Word. There is no doubt about it; they too had a set time they adhered to.

Now why am I saying this? I'm telling you that it's okay to have set times with the Lord. Regular attendance of structured church services is a good thing. Once again, set times are the rule, while being spontaneous is the exception. If it was good enough for the early disciples, it's surely good enough for us today.

Back to the Box

> ...God has set boundaries for us (a box, if
> you will) to keep us on the right track.

Some people say God wants them out of the box. While this sounds wonderful, the truth is that God has set boundaries for us (a box, if you will) to keep us on the right track. I do understand what people mean. They are trying to be open to the inspiration and leading of the Holy Ghost, but they take it to the extreme when they demand that all structure, form or set things be removed. They are trying to express the freedom found in Christ by saying, "I'm not religious anymore, and I'm not in anyone's box! I am free to do whatever I want to whomever I want! I am free!" This type of freedom seems more like an outward, man-made attempt to appear free while, at the same time, denying the power of God's Word.

If we look back to early times, we find that God put Adam and Eve in (yes, you guessed it) a box called the Garden of Eden. He also gave them a particularly boxy commandment, telling them what they should and should not eat. When they tried to get out of the box, the results were disastrous and far-reaching, affecting us even today.

> *This is the way the lampstand was made: it was a hammered work of gold, hammered from its base to its flower petals. The lampstand was made according to the pattern the Lord had shown Moses.* –NUMBERS 8:4

> *These serve as a copy and shadow of the heavenly things, as Moses was warned when he was about to complete the tabernacle. For God said, Be careful that you make everything according to the pattern that was shown to you on the mountain.* –HEBREWS 8:5

When God took the Israelites out of Egypt, He took them three days into the wilderness, and guess what He put them in? That's right—a box! He gave them instructions on building the tabernacle, saying, "Build this according to the pattern! Do not deviate from it!" Then He arranged them tribe-by-tribe, following a specific order and fashion. God expected them to stay within the boundaries He laid out.

> WHENEVER SOMETHING DOESN'T LINE UP WITH OUR
> SPIRITUAL IDEAS OR UNDERSTANDING, WE TEND TO CLASSIFY
> IT AS RELIGIOUS, OR HAVING A SPIRIT OF RELIGION.

The truth is this: being non-religious does not mean we throw out the rule book and do whatever feels good to us, nor is it based on what we perceive as religious. Just because we think it's so, doesn't make it so! Whenever something doesn't line up with our spiritual ideas or understanding, we tend to classify it as religious, or having a spirit of religion. True spiritual freedom from religion is not found in doing whatever we want. It is not permission to jump out of the box of God's Word and do whatever we think is spiritual. True freedom is the total opposite. To be free is to be empowered to live life according to God's Word. The Spirit of God and the Word of God will always agree.

Galatians 5:13 says, *"For you were called to be free, brothers; only don't use this freedom as an opportunity for the flesh, but serve one another through love."* Jesus lived His life by strict obedience to the law (Torah) and by the power of the Holy Spirit. His life of death-to-self is in direct contrast to the lifestyles of many of the so-called "led by the Spirit" people of the twenty-first century.

Spiritual freedom is a true test of character! What a person does when there are no boundaries will reveal who, or what, they are truly living for. Having the freedom to do whatever we want is not a good reason to step out of the boundaries. Instead, it should be about what God wants. From what we can see in Scripture, He wants us to stay in the box.

I'm not saying that we aren't to be innovative or imaginative in our approach to life, business, or ministry. I am merely stating that the box God wants us to stay in is the boundary of the Word of God. It is very easy to misapply the "out of the box" mentality, and without realizing it, step outside of His Word and His ways.

Enter at Your Own Risk

I think as quickly as people are trying to get out of their so called religious box, God is trying just as fast to put them back in. The deception of this thinking is that when we lose sight of life's God-given boundaries, be they natural or spiritual, we run the risk of entering what I call the "danger zone." This is an "enter at your own risk zone," where the boundaries have been crossed out, the protective fence has been breached or eliminated altogether, and trouble is not far away.

According to some people, being non-religious means stepping over the boundaries God has set before us and making life a free-for-all. It may sound innovative and progressive, but it is a warped view of what being religious really is.

I can testify to what jumping back into the box can do for a person or family. Years ago in my walk with the Lord, attending the regular services at church became an issue in my life. It became optional for me. If I felt like going, I went. If not, I stayed home. I cited spiritual freedom to combat the loud and clear disapproval coming from my conscience. Because I made church an option instead of the first priority, I was much weaker than I believed I was. I didn't want to be like that, but it was a difficult thing to overcome.

In 2000, I heard Steve Gray from World Revival Church speak about the dangers of living life with too many options. I was convicted and healed of my double-minded heart. I made the decision that I would never again give myself the option to do whatever I wanted. I put myself back into the box of set times for worship, prayer, and participation in regular church services and events. What relief that brought! Joy and strength came in after I decided that church attendance was no longer optional for me. The inner struggle vanished, and as for me and my house, we served the Lord. Our destiny as a family was put on the right track when I willingly went back into the "religious box" God designed for me to be in. As a result, our lives are better, our children love the Lord, and the fight is gone. Moreover, our whole church has become healthier in every way.

Consistent spiritual activity will produce consistent spiritual health.

The enemy is quickly defeated when we have a life with set times that are not optional. Consistent spiritual activity will produce consistent spiritual health. When we give ourselves too many options, we usually take them. The problem with these options is that they usually take us farther from God, not closer. They make us weaker rather than stronger. Many believers use their freedom to indulge their flesh, or use it as an excuse to justify lazy Christianity. We have even used our attempts to jump out of the box as a means to justify rebellion against the church, its structure, and form.

In 2 Timothy 3:5 Paul says, *"Holding to the form of godliness but denying its power. Avoid these people!"* I understand our fear of being religious, but for the most part, our anxieties are unwarranted. Some people are more concerned about looking religious to their peers than about the lordship of Christ in their lives. Instead of being afraid of appearing religious, we should fear the lack of God's presence and power in our lives. If you truly want to be non-religious, make sure God's presence and power are actually in your life, be it at church, at home, and in those spontaneous moments. *This is freedom from religion in its truest sense!*

9

WAS JESUS REALLY
A REBEL?

There was a time, as a new believer, when I was not very submissive or willing to follow leadership of any kind. Even though I went to church, I was still prone to doing things my own way (Those around me think I still do, but I'm working on it! LOL!), and I wasn't getting anywhere. I brought my rebellion and stubborn ways into my religion, but it wasn't bearing good fruit. I always growled to myself, "no one can tell me what to do," or, "who are they to speak into my life, after all, I have God too!" As you can imagine, things weren't panning out as I hoped. My rebellion was hindering my growth and ability to be blessed under another man's ministry and grace.

As I was walking and praying one night, God spoke these words to me: "Go to the church and submit to the pastors there. Do whatever they tell you and the next five years will be five of your best!" I obeyed and, indeed, the Word of the Lord came true. When I submitted myself, the grace of God came upon me. I learned a valuable lesson: there is safety in God's established system of authority, so why should I go against it?

SUBMISSION IS NOT DANGEROUS

True submission is a two way street. It isn't as one-sided as many suppose. A good leader will lead the flock by example, and because of this, the grace of God will be evident.

In the same way, you younger men, be subject to the elders. And all of you clothe yourselves with humility toward one another, because God resists the proud but gives grace to the humble. Humble yourselves, therefore, under the mighty hand of God, so that He may exalt you at the proper time, casting all your care on Him, because He cares about you. —1 PETER 5:5–7

Peter goes on to address the other side of the equation by saying, *"in the same way."* In the same way that the governing leaders walk with God in a submissive manner, so you should walk towards them. Be subject to the elders, for they are the spiritual leaders in the assembly you are a part of. All of us are to clothe ourselves with humility (submissiveness). God commanded everyone to submit one to another, and Peter explained why—*"God resists the proud but gives grace to the humble."*

... OUR SUBMISSION TO GOD IS MOST OFTEN REVEALED
THROUGH OUR WILLINGNESS TO YIELD TO MAN.

After Peter had been talking to the church about submission, it appears as if he changed to the topic of pride, but did he? No, he is still speaking in the context of submission, because God resists the proud. If I were to ask people if they felt they were submitted to God, would anyone answer no? I don't think so. We all believe we are submitted to God, but the truth is, our submission to God is most often revealed through our willingness to yield to man.

We could paraphrase it like this, "God resists those who refuse to submit, but gives grace to those who do." God gives grace to people who submit to man because of Jesus, who also submitted to man. Jesus, the creator, submitted Himself to the creation! If Jesus could submit to man, how come we struggle so much with it?

My life became drastically better after I submitted myself to the leadership of the church. I believed I was doing a great job in my life, being my own boss, and not being accountable to anyone else, but I was bearing bad fruit. When I submitted to leadership, the grace of God came into my life to a greater degree than it had been before. God promises more grace to those who submit to man's authority. I learned to submit to spiritual leadership, but what about natural leadership? Would I be as willing? Let's find out.

I began working for a major hotel chain. I started out in night security and worked my way up to night manager. It didn't pay much money, but God used that place to work out the rebellion and stubbornness I had accrued. After being there for six months, I was ushered into the manager's office where he proceeded to explain the results of his evaluation of my work ethics. I thought to myself, *I'll get an excellent report; after all, I have been a model employee. Go ahead, evaluate away!* It was going well until he said the words, "Now for the bad part." He began to inform me about some of my not-so-Christian traits. At that time, my attitude was, *I am a King's kid, so who are you to evaluate me? I am a believer, born again, a son of God, and I am the righteousness of God. How can you sit there and speak to me about my faults? You, of all people—a sinner!"* As if! Well, I listened to him, and when I left his office, I was self righteously upset. Who was he to judge me anyway? I didn't need his opinion; I only wanted God's opinion!

On the way home, however, the Spirit of the Lord gave me His opinion, and began to deal with my heart and attitude. He told me, in no uncertain terms as only He can, that my manager was correct and that what he had judged me to be was correct. That was so hard to hear. I had thought God was on my side! Well, He was on my side. He was using this company to work out some of my faults, one being a lack of submission to authority. I had always prided myself on my stubbornness, and even thought of it as a good trait. Was I ever deceived! The Lord spoke to me that day and asked me to submit to all authority, even if it came from the ungodly. God dealt with my rebellious heart, and I have never been the same since. I know God has blessed my life since that time.

Let me make one thing clear: I am not proud that God had to speak to me to bring me into line. I already knew from my knowledge of the Word that I was to submit to those in positions of authority. If God has to stand over us to get us to obey what He already told us to do in His Word, then that is not obedience. The highest form of obedience would be simply to read it and do it. In fact, if God has to talk us into doing what is right, then we cannot say we are spiritual but rather, rebellious.

That's not something to be proud of. We must always look at the context from which He is speaking. I thank God that He speaks to us, but I want Him to speak to me for vision, direction and spiritual insight, not to convict me for my disobedience.

JESUS —WAS HE REALLY REBELLIOUS?

So then, the law is holy, and the commandment is holy and just and good. –ROMANS 7:12

Let's take a closer look at Jesus. Was He rebellious toward His parents? Did He lead a rebellion against the authorities of the day? Did He break the law or uphold it? Does He ask us to rebel today? I don't believe so! I believe most of the rebellious attitudes in the church today are a direct result of the idea that our Lord was a rebel. We rebel because we believe He rebelled. We think we are doing what He did.

Many believe He was the epitome of rebellion, and came to rebel against the establishment, both naturally and spiritually. This belief has been our motivation to be a rabble-rouser, who comes against every type of authority, and is rebellious and stubborn. We even assume Jesus came to establish a form of rebellion against the current religious system and all natural governments. Wrong on both counts!

Some people are motivated by this false conception of Jesus, and they live it out in a lifestyle that is anti-everything, believing they are identifying with the Master! As a result, they continue to do their own thing, have no value for authority, and do that which is right in their own eyes.

Jesus didn't rebel against the Roman government as many of the Jews wanted Him to, nor did He come to replace the spiritual laws that God had set up in the first place. The law didn't need replacing; it was holy, just, and good. The problem was never the holy laws of God, but the corrupt hearts of the people.

Jesus instituted both spiritual and natural law, so why would He come and do away with them? While He certainly desired to remove the corruption from the religious system, He wasn't trying to replace it or rebel against it. Jesus was not a rebel!

*Behold my servant, whom I uphold, my chosen, in whom my soul
delights; I have put my Spirit upon him; he will bring forth justice
to the nations. He will not cry aloud or lift up his voice, Or make
it heard in the street;* –ISAIAH 42:1–2, ESV

He was not the initiator of an underground movement to overthrow
the Pharisees or the Romans. He didn't have secret meetings with the rebellious movements of that day, nor was He handing out anti-establishment literature everywhere He went. He didn't staple anti-government
papers on every post or tree, nor did He run an underground printing
press that published anti-Roman periodicals. He certainly wasn't partic-
ipating in any protest rallies.

Jesus wasn't at all like many think He was. He didn't have a false
sense of self-righteousness, thinking He was here on a special mission to
overthrow the governing authorities. He didn't have a sense of bravado,
where He saw Himself as the great liberator who would free the Israelites
from the Romans. He wasn't an arrogant loudmouth out in the streets,
using His spiritual greatness, power, or knowledge to beat everyone down.
He came for another reason: to bring justice to the nations through His
death, burial, and resurrection. He was the ultimate sacrifice.

Many want to mouth off today, spouting whatever they want in the
name of religion, self-righteousness or their dissatisfaction with the current system, but none of that will change anything. Only by following the
way of the Master can we hope to make a difference in this world.

JESUS CHANGED THE WORLD THROUGH HIS
GREAT HUMILITY, OBEDIENCE, AND SACRIFICE!

Was Jesus Rebellious Toward His Parents?

*Every year His parents traveled to Jerusalem for the Passover
Festival. When He was 12 years old, they went up according to
the custom of the festival.* –LUKE 2:41–42

As I previously stated, it might surprise some of you that Jesus was Jewish. He grew up obeying the Torah and observed all the feasts, statutes, and even some of the elders' traditions. He obeyed the Word by observing the Sabbath every Friday night, and He ate a full kosher diet. Contrary to many folks today, Jesus did not come to do away with the Torah, or the law; He came to fulfill it, live it out, and reveal it in its fullness. No Jew would have believed in Jesus as Messiah if He had disobeyed or dismissed the Torah.

> *After those days were over, as they were returning, the boy Jesus stayed behind in Jerusalem, but His parents did not know it. Assuming He was in the traveling party, they went a day's journey. Then they began looking for Him among their relatives and friends. When they did not find Him, they returned to Jerusalem to search for Him.* –LUKE 2:43–45

His parents didn't realize He had stayed behind. No doubt, up to this time, He had never given them cause for concern. After all, He was the sinless Messiah! He could never have been rebellious as a child or teenager. Any rebellion would have disqualified His case for being the Messiah.

They looked for Him among their relatives and friends who had travelled with them, but He wasn't there, so they turned around and went back. They finally found Him three days later, and what was He doing? He was asking questions and listening to the spiritual leaders in the temple. Wow! What kind of twelve year old boy was He? Think about it—a twelve year old doing what most adults struggle to do—asking and listening. After all, doesn't the Bible tell us to be quick to hear and slow to speak? Most people today would rather talk than listen. They want to be the person with all the answers. The church is full of these spiritual teenagers who think they are qualified to speak into other people's lives, yet still struggle to hear and be obedient to the Father and His leaders.

We have many who have never been in ministry, pastored a church, or had any experience in leading people, yet they are trying to speak into the lives of leadership. They believe they are mature, but in many ways are still wet behind the ears spiritually. Instead of being rebellious and having all the answers about church, they should be sitting at the feet of God's leadership asking questions and listening.

That is what Jesus did, and if we truly desire to be like Him, we should do what He did. Luke says, *"And all those who heard Him were astounded at His understanding and His answers"* (Luke 2:47).

Yes, Jesus astonished them with His understanding and maturity level, but never, ever, ever, did He think to rebel against those leaders. Even though He was only twelve, they allowed Him to listen and be a part of their discussions of Torah. That, my friends, tells us precisely the sort of guy Jesus was. He wasn't rebellious towards them at all. No doubt, He had some different explanations or understandings of Torah, but He didn't speak out in an arrogant, proud or rebellious manner.

> *When His parents saw Him, they were astonished, and His mother said to Him, "Son, why have You treated us like this? Your father and I have been anxiously searching for You."*
> —LUKE 2:48

Why were Joseph and Mary astonished at this? Perhaps it was the first time Jesus had ever engaged the leaders in Torah discussion. Maybe it was because He had never done anything to cause His parents concern before. They didn't understand what was going on. I love His reply:

> *"Why were you searching for Me?" He asked them. "Didn't you know that I had to be in My Father's house?" But they did not understand what He said to them.* —LUKE 2:49

We often read into Jesus' comments and conclude that He was being rebellious toward His parents, but He was merely explaining His actions. Jesus had a purpose, and it was time to get started in learning about the temple religion and the fullness of the Torah. He told them He was called to be engaged in His Father's affairs. It is very important that we recognize what was going on here. Jesus was beginning to grasp who and what He really was. I can imagine He was drawn to the temple and the leaders like Winnie the Pooh to honey. It is also likely that being in close proximity to the temple had an effect on Him; perhaps His heart was burning like never before.

Do you know what else He was doing there? He was learning. While many in our day are struggling to listen to the leadership in the church, Jesus had, on purpose, spent three days with these guys, asking, listening, and learning. They must have noticed something in Him that would motivate them to let Him stay for three days. I doubt this was a common practice; however, Jesus warranted that kind of attention, even at a young age.

When He spoke those words to His parents, they didn't understand Him. You see, He was starting to understand that He was to be about His Father's business. The fullness of the revelation of the Son of God had not yet been given, and He told them no more than this.

I love what happened next: *"Then He went down with them and came to Nazareth and was obedient to them. His mother kept all these things in her heart"* (Luke 2:51).

Look what Jesus did! He went home with His parents. He didn't start a new ministry as a result of His great revelations. He didn't take off to travel with a group of young people in a van. He didn't go off on a soul-searching adventure, nor did He think Himself too high and mighty to listen to His parents. He simply went home and was obedient to them. Carefully consider this: Jesus, the Son of God, equal to the Father and Holy Ghost, all things made by Him, through Him and for Him, was obedient to His earthly parents. The boy was in submission to the parents HE created. Yes, this Heavenly Father sent, Holy Ghost wrought, Son of the living God, went home and was perfectly compliant to two ordinary human beings, Joseph and Mary. Inconceivable, but true!

It's funny how the Son of God could be submitted to those in earthly authority over Him, yet we see people like ourselves struggling with it. Jesus didn't feel He was higher than the natural authorities the Father had placed Him under, and neither should we. The creator in submission to the creation—what a holy concept! What a great model of humility and submission for all of us to follow!

If Jesus could do it, then why is it that so many of us can't, or won't? Why could He be submissive and subject Himself to ordinary authorities while so many refuse today, even citing Jesus as the inspiration for their behaviour? It is wrong to think the rebellious are like Him in any way, shape, or form. Luke says, *"And Jesus increased in wisdom and stature, and in favor with God and with people"* (Luke 2:52).

Jesus was under the authority of God by being in submission to man. Yes, this can be abused, but for the most part, it isn't. Jesus was an example of doing it the right way. This is a principle many don't want to involve themselves with, but it is a godly one nonetheless and is highly beneficial to both parties. It is God's way! Because of Jesus' obedience, God granted Him great favour, and He increased in wisdom and stature.

Rebellion and stubbornness will decrease the stature you and I have with people and with God. People don't like to work with rebellion, and neither does God. If submission to authority increases wisdom and stature, then logically, a rebellious person will decrease in wisdom and stature. Do you want your wisdom and stature to increase or decrease?

WAS JESUS REBELLIOUS AS AN ADULT?

> *He will not cry aloud or lift up his voice, or make it heard in the street…* —ISAIAH 42:2, ESV

> *At that time Jesus said to the crowds, "Have you come out with swords and clubs, as if I were a criminal, to capture Me? Every day I used to sit, teaching in the temple complex, and you didn't arrest Me. But all this has happened so that the prophetic Scriptures would be fulfilled." Then all the disciples deserted Him and ran away.* —MATTHEW 26:55–56

Jesus wasn't in the streets causing riots or trouble like Barabbas was. He was often in the temple and the synagogues, preaching and teaching for all to hear. He didn't have a hidden ministry, where He skulked around behind the leader's back, speaking negatively and criticizing. No, He was up front, in their face, and accountable to them all. There was no darkness in Him! None!

Today, many do all of their preaching and teaching in darkness, not willing to be accountable for what they say. They say it quite boldly in the corner or through the medium of Facebook, emails, or letters. They usually don't do it in public, where they can be held accountable or judged for what they are saying. Jesus always spoke in front of the temple leaders. He was the light of the world; how could He hide in darkness?

NOTHING DONE SECRETLY

> The high priest questioned Jesus about his disciples and about his teaching. "I have spoken openly to the world," Jesus answered him. "I have always taught in the synagogue and in the temple complex, where all the Jews congregate, and I haven't spoken anything in secret. Why do you question Me? Question those who heard what I told them. Look, they know what I said." –JOHN 18:19–21

Jesus wasn't the secretive type, and He didn't have a hidden agenda. He was always authentic in public and didn't hide His thoughts or motives. He didn't have secret meetings with Barabbas to plan revolts or initiate riots in the streets to bolster His cause. He spoke openly to the Jews so they could hear every word. He always faced those who were in opposition to Him.

Many people prefer to do things in secret these days. They are loud and proud on Internet media, but rarely do they give anyone the opportunity to critique their words. Those who try are labeled as religious or out of date. They alone seem to have the "Word of the Lord" for today, yet they seem to do all their speaking in secret, never in the presence of the local church or leadership. Jesus did none of this!

My feeling is this: if you can't say it in front of everyone, should you be saying anything at all? Because of the wonderful media resources in our grasp today, many are becoming Internet prophets, speaking where there is no accountability or responsibility for what they say. It is so easy to write whatever one feels from a computer, but not so easy when it is done under the scrutiny of church leadership. I guess that is why they do it! If Jesus spoke openly, allowing the leaders and the people to hear, then shouldn't we do the same?

SPEAKING OUT OF TURN NOW MAY COST
THEM THEIR SAY IN THE FUTURE.

I believe there are many who are called to speak to the church world, but some of them are speaking prematurely. They have a glimpse of the message they are to speak, but their character and message has not fully developed yet. It would be best if they stayed silent for now and grew in maturity and wisdom. Then maybe, just maybe, God will use them later on. Speaking out of turn now may cost them their say in the future.

Jesus obviously knew who He was and what He was going to do, but He didn't begin speaking openly until He was thirty years of age. He waited many years before opening His mouth. Just because you have a mouth, doesn't mean you should open it! My wife often tells me, "Brent, just because you think it doesn't mean you should say it!" As Mark Twain said, "It is better to keep your mouth closed and let people think you are a fool than to open it and remove all doubt."

ILLEGITIMATE AUTHORITY

> *And no one takes this honor for himself, but only when called by God, just as Aaron was.* –HEBREWS 5:4, ESV

Even Aaron could not take the priestly mantle upon himself; it had to be given to him by God. Some of you who are reading this may be thinking, *The leaders don't recognize my calling or gifting, so I will just do it on my own.* If God wants you to speak for Him, He will make a way, and it will be done in cooperation with man. Anyone who takes it upon himself to do it without man's permission becomes an illegitimate spiritual authority. Many people might not like that, but it is the truth. It is better to work with man than to work against him. Remember: God is a co-labourer with man!

The problem that keeps cropping up in the church world today is a lack of trust in God. People want to point the finger of blame at man, but the truth is that only God can make us into what He wants us to be. If He wants you in a public ministry, He will work it out, have no fear. We have to understand that God will also speak to leadership to confirm someone's call to the public arena of ministry. It's time to trust God to see your calling fulfilled, instead of trying to make it happen on your own.

In another chapter, we discussed serving in the church as deacons and how they needed to be proven before being given a position. If a deacon must first be proved, then how much more for someone called into full time, public ministry? In the book of Acts, when a problem came up concerning the distribution and serving of food to the widows, requirements were necessary. They chose seven men, full of the Holy Ghost and faith, who were of a good reputation. Those were quite the qualifications just to wait on tables, yet in today's church, people are propelling themselves forward faster than a speeding bullet, unproven and not caring who endorses them.

If Jesus was walking on the earth in fleshly form today, He would not be joining these people; instead, you would find Him being faithful and submissive to the current spiritual leadership, because He is not a rebel!

People often forget there are a lot of factors thrown into the equation when it comes to the release of giftings and callings. We want to run out there and be God's voice to the nations, but He isn't in nearly as much of a hurry as we are. Relax, take the time to learn, grow, and overcome all rebellion in your life so God can make the most of you when the time comes. Even Jesus didn't rush to walk out His ministry; there was a set time to be released into it. He spent thirty years submitting, learning, growing, and maturing before God's mantle came upon Him to do His will.

If you don't do it the right way, people will not likely listen to what you have to say. The more we are submitted to man, the more they are apt to listen to us. Jesus did it the right way, shouldn't you? *"And if you have not been faithful in that which is another's, who will give you that which is your own?"* (Luke 16:12, ESV).

The place where we are proven or tested is in another person's ministry. Faithfulness to someone else is one of the ways to become qualified for our own ministry. This is not just about being a faithful person, but being totally faithful to someone other than yourself. It is about listening, learning, growing, being involved, and yes, even being corrected from time to time.

If you struggle with faithfulness to another man, who will be faithful to you, should you gain a ministry in the future? *"Don't be deceived: God is not mocked. For whatever a man sows, he will also reap"* (Galatians 6:7).

Many are called, but few are chosen, because they fail this faithfulness test. They fail to prove themselves in the eyes of man and God. They have believed a lie that says, "I only have to prove myself to God, and He knows my heart." While this may sound good and spiritual, it is not the whole truth of the matter. The Scriptures are quite clear on this, but people like to twist them to justify their own thinking. Luke states, *"As for that in the good soil, they are those who, hearing the word, hold it fast in an honest and good heart, and bear fruit with patience"* (Luke 8:15, ESV).

If we truly want to be like Jesus, then we must follow His example. He was submitted and faithful to His parents, elders, religious leaders, and finally, to the Father Himself. He grew in stature and favour with God and man.

The seed of God's Word cannot flourish in the tainted soil of rebellion.

Rebellion stifles the spiritual growth of those who operate in it. Rebels will not grow in spiritual stature. Instead of maturing or growing in spiritual things, they will actually begin to digress. It isn't possible to grow spiritually when operating out of a spirit or heart of rebellion. Spiritual growth comes to those who have a good and honest heart. The seed of God's Word cannot flourish in the tainted soil of rebellion.

Notice it says, *"With a good, honest and patient heart."* Sometimes people rebel merely because they are impatient. They are in a hurry and want to speed it up, so the standard process is disregarded in favour of the fast track to ministry. I think many people believe those who are called to ministry would never even try to rebel, but the truth is that much of the rebellion being displayed is from those who are called to the ministry. They have mistakenly viewed their calling as the right to speak on any level, even against current spiritual leadership. James explains, *"Not many of you should become teachers, my brothers, for you know that we who teach will be judged with greater strictness"* (James 3:1, ESV).

I don't think this principle is understood fully within the body of believers as a whole. We must not forget that those who are in the place of public ministry will be scrutinized and judged on a stricter scale than the average believer. It is a serious thing to speak out without submitting to some kind of spiritual authority who will hear and judge what is said. They can bring correction if necessary, and also encouragement, help, and instruction to become a better communicator.

I remember the first time I was given the privilege to speak in front of our church. I received about two weeks notice, and for that whole time I was a nervous wreck! The good news about being scared is you tend to spend a lot of time preparing and praying! They introduced me, and with fear and trepidation, I walked up the aisle and climbed the four steps to the pulpit. My legs were shaking, my heart was racing, and believe me when I say I was sweating as if I had run a marathon. It took about ten minutes for the nervousness to go away and for my voice to settle down. That was many years ago, and since that time, I haven't lost any of that nervousness, and I think that is a good thing. You don't want to become too good at speaking that you forget it is an awesome and sacred privilege to speak for God to His people. It is not something anyone should take lightly.

When it was finally over I was filled with tremendous relief. I remember some of the older ladies coming up to me afterwards and giving me words of encouragement, saying, "You did so well," or "That was really helpful." I knew what they actually meant was, "You really stunk, but we love you anyway!" I am thankful for those ladies who were such an encouragement to me, even though I knew my preaching wasn't that great.

There was one sweet, little East Indian lady, God bless her soul, who would come and love me by slapping me in the face a few times. For some reason, this was her way of showing encouragement and approval. I took it all in stride, knowing she loved me.

JESUS BEAT THEM AT THEIR OWN GAME

Let the righteous smite me; it shall be a kindness: and let him reprove me; it shall be excellent oil, which shall not break my head: for yet my prayer also shall be in their calamities. –PSALM 141:5, KJV

I am thankful for the people around me who gave me advice and instruction, as well as my pastor, who challenged me to speak in love and always think about the audience, remembering it is to them that I speak. Public ministry isn't about the person speaking, but about a God-called, and anointed person delivering His oracles for the benefit of the hearers. Too many begin to use whatever avenues they can find to speak and lift themselves up, with no regard for the people. They are eager to share their revelations, ideas or teachings, believing they are called of God outside of normal spiritual authority. People who believe they are outside the norms of spiritual authority will do whatever they want with no consideration of what anyone else thinks. This is rebellion! Some people say, "Well, Jesus did whatever He wanted to do!"

Did Jesus do whatever He wanted? I don't think so. I think He used wisdom to operate within the system He created and knew so well. Let me help you by telling you a story. Some years ago my wife and I bought a house from a guy, let's call him Tom, who does a lot of business in the city of Saskatoon. He is very successful because he learned how to operate within the parameters and guidelines set out by the city officials. Before we purchased the house from him, we had to rent it for a time. One day, the doorbell rang, and the city taxman wanted to come in and do an assessment of the house. He was all smiles as he asked if I owned the house. I told him no, and when I said who did, his expression instantly changed from happiness to frustration. He said, "Oh, I hate that guy!" At that time, I wondered what he meant.

In the years that followed, I spent time with Tom and he shared his strategy for working with the city. He decided that to beat the city at its own game he must learn the rules and regulations and become better acquainted with them than the city officials were. So now, whenever Tom does a project, he already knows what he can and cannot do according to the city's own regulations. You see, he learned the system better than the city personnel had, and was able to get what he wanted done. All the red tape and bureaucracy mattered little to him. He studied the building laws and was able to use them to their fullest extent. I call that genius, and I believe this is what Jesus did when He walked the earth. He may have come across as looking like He did whatever He wanted, whenever

He wanted, but all He did was play by the rules better than everyone else. To the untrained or unlearned, it might have appeared as if He was doing His own thing, but they didn't know what He knew.

The Jewish people were waiting for a Messiah to come as a conquering hero who would overthrow Rome, but Jesus came as a suffering servant who submitted to Roman authority. Because His actions and statements contradicted their expectations of how the Messiah would behave, Jesus was misunderstood then; and He still is today.

As you can see, Jesus didn't do whatever He wanted. He only did what His Father told Him, which was already established in the Law. While Jesus did correct certain misunderstandings and man-made traditions within first century Judaism, He wasn't trying to redefine the whole system. He operated within it and always showed respect for the religious authorities. Jesus wouldn't have divided His own Kingdom, for if He had, it would not have stood.

THE PROBLEM ISN'T THE SYSTEM IN ANY AGE,
BUT THE HEARTS OF THE PEOPLE WITHIN IT.

Corruption ran rampant in the religious system of Jesus' day, just as it does today. Changes definitely need to be made, but let's keep in mind that being rebellious isn't God's way of implementing them. Jesus played by the rules and so should we! Two wrongs have never made a right! Just because some people within the modern day religious system are corrupt, it doesn't mean everyone is. The problem isn't the system in any age, but the hearts of the people within it. If we are going to implement change, then let's do it without rebelling, for in our rebellion, we prove ourselves more wrong than right. The end doesn't justify the means!

There are people who desire to bring about change, and I believe many of them are meant to do so, but they need to go about it correctly *within* the system, having first gained the respect of those functioning in it. While it is one thing to speak, it is quite another to get people to listen! I want to encourage those who long to see change to go about it with total submission to the spiritual authorities around them. In this way, changes can happen without operating in a spirit of rebellion. Sometimes the people who want change the most develop a bad attitude, and say all the right things, but because of their attitude, no one is listening. Just seeing what needs to be changed won't do anything until the people will listen to what you have to say. A person can have the greatest of revelations, but if the people aren't interested in what is being said, it will have little or no impact. People don't want to know how much you know until they know how much you care!

Good and honest believers can smell a bad attitude ten miles away. If they sense a rebellious attitude, they will not hear it. There are people who are seeing what needs to be changed in religion, but their methods leave a lot to be desired. A person can be sincere in what they are saying, but be sincerely wrong. Likewise, a person can be saying what is right, but because of a rebellious attitude, no one is willing to listen to them. You might be talking, but who is listening?

God is not into rebellion. The devil is the one who operates in it—not God, not Jesus, and not the Holy Ghost! Jesus bore the sin of our rebellion when He was nailed to the cross. He absolutely crushed the power of rebellion by this unselfish act of love. As a result, people can be set completely free from its deadly evil, and serve with a heart attitude of submission, humility, and grace.

10

DID JESUS
REBEL AGAINST
THE LAW?

At that time Jesus passed through the grainfields on the Sabbath.
His disciples were hungry and began to pick and eat some heads
of grain. But when the Pharisees saw it, they said to Him, "Look,
Your disciples are doing what is not lawful to do on the Sabbath!"
—MATTHEW 12:1–2

Much of what I call "Christian rebellion" seems to stem from the idea that Jesus rebelled against the religious system of His day. This, in turn, tends to empower people today to do the same, and they truly think they are identifying with the rebellion of Jesus. It appears we need to discover what Jesus was really doing and why.

Was He revolting against the very law He gave? Could He be in opposition to His own Word? Did Jesus break the law by working on the Sabbath? It certainly looked like it. The religious crowds were very concerned about proper observance of Sabbath laws, and they constantly accused Jesus of breaking the law because He healed and delivered people on that day.

Work was prohibited on the Sabbath. First-century rabbis divided labour into thirty-nine categories, each having many subcategories. Three of the things prohibited were picking, threshing, and winnowing. The disciples picked grain and rubbed it between their hands to remove the husks and thus, they broke the highly restrictive rabbinic law on three different counts.

*He said to them, "Haven't you read what David did when he
and those who were with him were hungry—how he entered the
house of God, and they ate the sacred bread, which is not lawful
for him or for those with him to eat, but only for the priests? Or
haven't you read in the Law that on Sabbath days the priests in
the temple violate the Sabbath and are innocent? But I tell you
that something greater than the temple is here! If you had known
what this means: I desire mercy and not sacrifice, you would not
have condemned the innocent. For the Son of Man is Lord of the
Sabbath." –*MATTHEW 12:3–7

When you read verses where Jesus appeared to be doing away with
the law, resist the urge to believe it. He wasn't doing away with any of it.
He was merely explaining it to bring greater revelation.

When we read that the Pharisees said He was breaking the Sabbath, is that the truth, the whole truth, and nothing but the truth, so help
me God? No! What they accused him of and what actually happened
were two different things.

In verse 6, Jesus said, "...*something greater than the temple is here.*"
What was greater than the temple? One can read this and assume the
greater one is Jesus and conclude that He could break His own laws if
He chose. Is that correct? Would He decide to be in rebellion toward
His own law? No, He was saying that the preservation of a life was more
valuable than keeping the commandment.

Jesus gave them two examples from the Torah that supported His
point that preserving life was greater than temple law:

1. *The priests made and ate the consecrated bread (Leviticus
   24:5–8). The baking of the bread constituted work.*

2. *David and his men ate the consecrated bread, which normally
   only the priests could eat (1 Samuel 21:6).*

And he said to them, "Which of you, having a son or an ox that has fallen into a well on a Sabbath day, will not immediately pull him out?" —LUKE 14:5, ESV

Jesus had just healed a man on the Sabbath, and it sparked the usual controversy that He was breaking the law. Jesus explained that the preservation of life (even the life of an animal) took precedence over the keeping of the Sabbath rest. As you read about instances where Jesus allowed His disciples to disregard the law (the oral laws, the way Torah was to be lived out), don't assume He did this with all of the law. No, Jesus obeyed the law implicitly, except in cases where breaking it would save a life or help Him explain it better and bring the people greater revelation of how to walk it out.

Jesus said, *"Don't assume that I came to destroy the Law or the Prophets. I did not come to destroy but to fulfill"* (Matthew 5:17).

What did Jesus mean when He said He did not intend to destroy, but fulfill the Torah? Many have fatally assumed He meant to do away with the Torah (law) by being the fulfillment of it Himself. The Greek word, *pleroo*, means "to make full, to fill or full up." To fulfill the Torah is to obey it fully. Jesus came to fully obey the Torah. He didn't come to do away with the law, but to obey it perfectly, as only He could have done.

For I assure you: Until heaven and earth pass away, not the smallest letter or one stroke of a letter will pass from the law until all things are accomplished. Therefore, whoever breaks one of the least of these commands and teaches people to do so will be called least in the kingdom of heaven. But whoever practices and teaches these commands will be called great in the kingdom of heaven.
—MATTHEW 5:18–19

Jesus could no more have broken one of the commandments, no matter how insignificant, than He could have disobeyed the Father Himself. If He had, He never would have been accepted by any Jew as the Messiah, for the Messiah was to be sinless and perfect. However, when we read these accounts of eating on the Sabbath, not washing hands, or healing on the Sabbath, we think of Jesus as being a rebel who was breaking the laws of God. Not so! What Jesus did was fulfill the law in a better, more complete and perfect way. God declares, *"Keep My statutes and ordinances; a person will live if he does them. I am Yahweh"* (Leviticus 18:5).

Both Jesus and His disciples did things on the Sabbath that many considered to be labour, such as healing people and picking grain. This greatly upset the religious leaders. Jesus defended their actions by fully explaining the true extent of the heart of God. The idea is that the law was created to give life, not to endanger it. So then, the law must always be interpreted using the question, "Was life saved, or someone helped when you broke the Sabbath rest?"

> *Woe to you, scribes and Pharisees, hypocrites! You pay a tenth of mint, dill, and cumin, yet you have neglected the more important matters of the law—justice, mercy, and faith. These things should have been done without neglecting the others.* –MATTHEW 23:23

Jesus was displeased with those who felt the ceremonial laws were of greater importance than the moral laws. This verse proves in the strongest possible fashion that Jesus never considered annulling the law (even the ceremonial laws) and setting up a new one of His own.

What Jesus was trying to teach was that while it was right for them to obey the law concerning the tithe (which they did to the extreme), they weren't obeying it in the weightier things, like mercy, judgment, and love. Jesus certainly wasn't trying to replace one with the other. He wanted them to obey it all.

> *And as he entered a village, he was met by ten lepers, who stood at a distance and lifted up their voices, saying, "Jesus, Master, have mercy on us." When he saw them he said to them, "Go and show yourselves to the priests." And as they went they were cleansed.*
> –LUKE 17:12–14, ESV

*And behold, a leper came to him and knelt before him, saying,
"Lord, if you will, you can make me clean." And Jesus stretched
out his hand and touched him, saying, "I will; be clean." And
immediately his leprosy was cleansed. And Jesus said to him, "See
that you say nothing to anyone, but go, show yourself to the priest
and offer the gift that Moses commanded, for a proof to them."*
                                        —MATTHEW 8:2–4, ESV

These are two excellent examples of Jesus operating in full obedience to the Torah. He was being obedient to the law of Leviticus 14:2–
3a, which states, *"This is the law concerning the person afflicted with a skin
disease on the day of his cleansing. He is to be brought to the priest, who will
go outside the camp and examine him…"*

I am saying all this to help us understand that Jesus wasn't rebellious towards the law of God. How could He be? Would He come and
break His own Word, His own law, the very one given to the people of
God on Mount Sinai? It sounds counterproductive to think Jesus would
shoot Himself in the foot like that, doesn't it?

TRADITIONS OF MEN

*Then Pharisees and scribes came from Jerusalem to Jesus and
asked, "Why do Your disciples break the tradition of the elders?
For they don't wash their hands when they eat!" He answered
them, "And why do you break God's commandment because
of your tradition? For God said: Honor your father and your
mother; and, The one who speaks evil of father or mother
must be put to death. But you say, 'Whoever tells his father or
mother, "Whatever benefit you might have received from me is
a gift committed to the temple"—he does not have to honor his
father.' In this way, you have revoked God's word because of your
tradition." —MATTHEW 15:1–6*

When the religious leaders confronted Jesus because His disciples
didn't wash according to their traditions, He did what He does best;

He turned it around by asking them the same question: *"You accuse my disciples of breaking the traditions, but I am accusing you of breaking God's commandments."* In this case, the religious leaders were putting the tradition of giving a gift to the temple over the requirement of honouring their parents with financial support. They used this tradition as an excuse not to honour their parents as the law required. In truth, they were being greedy! They used this custom as a means to justify their love of money.

Jesus was reminding them of their obligation to obey the Torah by honouring their parents. Jesus obeyed the law and asked His people to do so, as well. Nowhere can we find an instance where Jesus disobeyed the law; He was obedient to it in its fullness.

WHAT ABOUT CIVIL LAW?

> *Then the Pharisees went and plotted how to trap Him by what He said. They sent their disciples to Him, with the Herodians. "Teacher," they said, "we know that You are truthful and teach truthfully the way of God. You defer to no one, for You don't show partiality. Tell us, therefore, what You think. Is it lawful to pay taxes to Caesar or not?"* –MATTHEW 22:15–17

Normally, the Pharisees and the Herodians didn't associate with each other, or agree on very many issues, but they were joining together for a common cause—hatred for Jesus. They felt He was a threat to the positions they held so dear and clung tightly to.

The Herodians were afraid that if Jesus came into power, Rome would be overthrown, and they would lose their prestigious positions. On the other hand, the Pharisees wanted Jesus to side with the Herodians, making him guilty by association. We need to remember that the common belief during this time was that the Messiah would come and be the conquering hero, who would dethrone the Romans and restore God's Kingdom in Israel. If He showed favour to Rome, it would have disqualified Him in their eyes as the Messiah, and the Jews would have abandoned Him.

The Pharisees hatched a plot to put Jesus in a difficult position by asking Him a controversial question with the Herodians present as witnesses. The question, *"Is it lawful to pay taxes to Caesar or not,"* was designed to put Jesus into an extremely dicey position. If He answered "no," He risked being accused of rebellion against Rome. If He answered "yes," He could be accused of supporting Roman oppression.

They started out first with the statement, *"We know that You are truthful and teach truthfully the way of God. You defer to no one for You don't show partiality."* They believed what people believe today—that Jesus deferred to no one and did whatever He wanted. This is an erroneous belief! While it is true that He is an impartial judge, who is above all human authority, Jesus willingly placed Himself under both civil and spiritual authority, as His response clearly indicated : *"But perceiving their malice, Jesus said, 'Why are you testing Me, hypocrites?'"* (Matthew 22:18).

Fully aware of their malicious intentions, Jesus brought forth His great wisdom to escape their scrutiny—unscathed and justified. He called people hypocrites, vipers, white washed tombs, and blind fools. I love Jesus, don't you? He had a knack for name calling like no one else. You can always tell when He was perturbed by their hypocrisy when he made use of name-calling. When He called them names, you knew He was quite upset. By the way, hypocrisy doesn't just describe a contradiction between reality and appearance. In this case, it was used to describe people who misinterpreted God's will and led people astray.

> *"Show Me the coin used for the tax."* So they brought Him a *denarius. "Whose image and inscription is this?"* He asked them. *"Caesar's,"* they said to Him. —MATTHEW 22:19–21a

When Jesus asked to see the coin used for taxes, they gave Him a denarius, the common Roman currency. In AD 6, Jewish revolutionaries had violently protested the use of such coins and incurred terrible Roman retaliation. The Pharisees hated what the coin represented, but still used it willingly in their day-to-day lives. How hypocritical was that! Again, they were testing Jesus to see whether He was loyal to Rome, or to His own people. He then inquired about whose image was inscribed on the coin, and they replied that it was a likeness of Caesar.

> Then He said to them, "Therefore give back to Caesar the things that are Caesar's, and to God the things that are God's." When they heard this, they were amazed. So they left Him and went away. —MATTHEW 22:21b–22

Jesus surprised them with His answer. When they heard it, they were amazed! They had not judged Him correctly at all. Because they believed He deferred to no one, they assumed they could use that knowledge against Him. Like so many today, they thought Jesus was rebellious toward authority. Those tricksters didn't know Him at all! Jesus was submissive to all civil law, and this speaks volumes for us today. If anyone had the right to disobey Caesar and all of Rome, it was Jesus, but He never did.

> When they arrived in Capernaum, the collectors of the half shekel [the temple tax] went up to Peter and said, Does not your Teacher pay the half shekel? He answered, Yes. And when he came home, Jesus spoke to him [about it] first, saying, What do you think, Simon? From whom do earthly rulers collect duties or tribute— from their own sons or from others not of their own family? And when Peter said, From other people not of their own family, Jesus said to him, Then the sons are exempt. However, in order not to give offense and cause them to stumble [that is, to cause them to judge unfavorably and unjustly] go down to the sea and throw in a hook. Take the first fish that comes up, and when you open its mouth you will find there a shekel. Take it and give it to them to pay the temple tax for Me and for yourself.
> —MATTHEW 17:24–27, AMP

Here we see that Jesus had no equal. No one was higher on the authority scale, yet He chose to submit by paying the temple tax. The temple, by its very existence, was the physical representation of God on the earth, and Jesus implemented it. He created all things and all things were created for Him. In truth, all taxes should have been paid to Jesus.

Jesus explained His own position of authority to Peter. Being a son and not a stranger, He was free to do whatever He chose, but so as not to offend, He would pay the tax. He instructed Peter to go fishing, and in a fish, he would find what was needed and pay the taxes. What is going on? Jesus was the Son that should not have had to pay the temple tax, but He paid it willingly. He did what so many of us try not to do—pay taxes. Jesus submitted to an authority that had no legitimate jurisdiction over Him. Not quite the picture of a rebel, is it?

> *Be subject for the Lord's sake to every human institution, whether it be to the emperor as supreme, or to governors as sent by him to punish those who do evil and to praise those who do good. For this is the will of God, that by doing good you should put to silence the ignorance of foolish people. Live as people who are free, not using your freedom as a cover-up for evil, but living as servants of God.*
> —1 Peter 2:13–16, ESV

Jesus didn't use His freedom to express His own selfishness, arrogance, or pride.

Jesus didn't use His freedom to express His own selfishness, arrogance, or pride. Instead, He gave us a picture of what true authority really is. It is humility that submits to every human institution on the earth. Jesus, man's creator, chose to humble Himself and submit to His own creation's authority. Interestingly, Jesus had no problem doing what most of mankind struggles with—submission to someone else. The most common temptation of people who are given greater authority is to use it to do whatever they want, claiming freedom as their justification. Jesus, on the other hand, used His freedom to humble Himself and walk in submission to the people He was in authority over. Jesus showed us what true humility and submission look like, and it is quite different from the way most of us see it.

Jesus could have gotten all riled up and ranted, "You don't know who I am, do you? I am the one who made all this! You should be paying taxes to Me!" Instead, He lowered Himself to meet their requirements. What an awesome man He was! Perhaps we can learn a lesson or two about true humility and submission from the greatest example of all time.

INSTEAD OF USING REBELLION, JESUS BROUGHT TRUE
FREEDOM THROUGH THE AVENUE OF SUBMISSION.

As you can see, Jesus never took issue with the Roman government and was misunderstood for it. Most people believed the Messiah would come as a conquering hero and deliver the nation of Israel. He did come as a conquering hero, just not in the way they were expecting. Instead of using rebellion, Jesus brought true freedom through the avenue of submission.

HYPOCRITICAL LEADERSHIP

> *Then Jesus spoke to the crowds and to His disciples: "The scribes and the Pharisees are seated in the chair of Moses. Therefore do whatever they tell you, and observe it. But don't do what they do, because they don't practice what they teach."* —MATTHEW 23:1–3

Scripture doesn't permit us to rebel against constituted authorities just because they don't live it perfectly. On the contrary, we are told to listen to them even if they do wrong, but not to copy their example.

When Jesus did things contrary to the religious leaders, He wasn't coming across as a rebel who was defying them because they had misinterpreted the law. No, He lived it better than they did! Many want to attack spiritual or natural leadership on the earth, but they, themselves, never rise to the occasion and live it out in a better way. Christianity is full of disgruntled people who are tired of hypocritical leadership. You can find quotes and comments all over media outlets such as TV, magazines, Facebook, and so on. It's easy to criticize, but how many are living it better than the ones they're accusing?

If we don't like something, we shouldn't just yack about it. We should try to live it out better by fully obeying the Word. I have had people tell me they won't go to church because it is full of hypocrites. They seem to feel justified saying, "At least I'm not being a hypocrite by going to church when I know full well I'm not perfect." While this sounds valiant and honourable, it is far from it. We can't stop obeying the Word because we are incapable of living it perfectly. *Au contraire*, we continue to do the best we can, knowing we are not perfect, but trying to be obedient to the best of our understanding.

USING THE HYPOCRISY OF CHURCH MEMBERS TO JUSTIFY
YOUR OWN DISOBEDIENCE WILL NEVER CUT IT WITH JESUS.

We are all hypocrites to some extent. None of us are able to live perfectly as Jesus did, but we must not give up. Using the hypocrisy of church members to justify our own disobedience will never cut it with Jesus.

Jesus didn't break the law, nor did He teach others to do so! He was a fully Torah observant Jew who dressed, spoke, and lived His life in obedience to the law. If we time-traveled back to the first century, I dare say that most of us wouldn't be able to pick Him out of a gathering of religious leaders. I've said all of this to help us understand that because Jesus wasn't rebellious to spiritual authority, we shouldn't be either.

Jesus is our greatest example of a person who was not rebellious. He paid all taxes required, gave honour to whom honour was due, and obeyed all the laws of the land. He did differ in His interpretation of some of the laws, but that is to be expected; after all, He was God in the flesh. Who better than Jesus to unveil the true meaning of the Torah to His people?

> *Everyone must submit to the governing authorities, for there is no authority except from God, and those that exist are instituted by God. So then, the one who resists the authority is opposing God's command, and those who oppose it will bring judgment on themselves.* —ROMANS 13:1–2

If we really and truly want to be identified with the Master, then we must do away with any rebellion in our lives. Jesus was not rebellious! I can't emphasize this enough. He didn't teach anyone to disobey the laws of God, nor did He instruct people to disregard the authority and teachings of those in spiritual leadership. He would never have considered this option because it would disqualify Him in their eyes as the Messiah. Jesus wasn't the originator of spiritual rebellion, nor was He anti-establishment or anti-authority.

Jesus was the perfect model of total submission to the Word of God ever to walk the face of the earth. If we desire to be like Jesus, then our goal should be to live as He lived, walk as He walked, and obey as He obeyed. If we rebel against the spiritual authority in our lives, are we not living in total opposition to our Lord? How could the One who wrote the law be found guilty of disregarding it?

True identification with Jesus can't be found in rebellion. If you want to be true to Him, then I would encourage you to walk as He did, one hundred percent yielded to His Father, to His Word and to the authorities He, Himself, instituted. As you do, God's grace and favour will be yours!

11.

Rebellion's
END

Rebellion Cannot Bear Good Fruit

U nfortunately, there is an outcome to rebellion that no one
wants to discuss, but we must. If left unchecked, rebellion will
continue to produce what the enemy sowed into Adam and
Eve so many years ago—disobedience, calamity, and destruction. If we
allow ourselves to rebel in any manner, we are working for the kingdom
of darkness instead of the Kingdom of God.

It is extremely easy to get caught up in rebellion, even to the point of
being unaware that we are operating in it. Rebellion is so widespread that
it appears to be today's normal behaviour. It is so common that people
almost expect others to be rebellious. Because doing the right thing is so
rare, people who try to follow the rules or walk in a yielded, submissive
manner are often considered weird or strange.

Take children or teens, for example. When they are submissive and
yielded, people will comment on how good they are. Just recently, a friend
of mine took his daughter with him to a local coffee shop and the manager commented, "Your daughter is so well behaved. I see so many kids
in here, and let me tell you, this is unusual." She was so impressed, she
bought them a treat, and he was able to share with her about the Lord.

We must always remember that God is totally against rebellion of
every kind, even at the minutest level. In believers, it should be extremely
difficult to find, but sadly, that isn't the case. It seems rebellion is alive and
well on Planet Church! Paul says, *"For the mystery of lawlessness (rebellion)*

is already at work, but the one now restraining will do so until he is out of the way" (2 Thessalonians 2:7, emphasis added).

The influence of rebellion is already at work. It's in the air, the people, the community; it's everywhere! It would be difficult to find a place or a people where rebellion wasn't found.

Consider the workplace. It's easy to act like everyone else in the office or at the job site. When a person speaks against the boss, or complains about something, isn't it the easiest thing to nod in agreement, or voice our displeasure? We can be so quick to offer our opinions or speak against someone else because it's going on all around us. You can go anywhere in the world and find this spirit at work in people. Like it or not, we have all been exposed to rebellious attitudes, and we must fight against them on a daily basis. After all, "one bad apple can spoil the whole bunch."

FAMILIARITY BREEDS CONTEMPT

Miriam and Aaron criticized Moses because of the Cushite woman he married. –NUMBERS 12:1

Familiarity can be a catalyst for rebellion. Aaron and Miriam felt that their close family connection to Moses justified their criticism of his actions. They thought they had a legitimate beef with him because he had married a Cushite woman. It is assumed by many scholars that this woman was of a different ethnic background. That could have been the cause for Miriam and Aaron's concern, although God was never against interracial marriages. He was only concerned if the interracial marriage brought idol worship into the union.

This is a common thread among rebellion in mankind. When Moses' family saw what they considered to be unrighteousness in their brother, rebellion was given an atmosphere in which to flourish. This is why rebellion can appear almost godly in nature. It is empowered by perceived unrighteousness. It takes the attitude that as long as I think the leader is up to snuff, I will follow, but if I see a chink in his armour, then something needs to change. What we forget is that God does not call people to lead because they are perfect, but rather because it is His will.

It isn't based solely on qualifications that fit the eye of man. God looks on the inward, while man tends to look on the outward.

What motivated Miriam and Aaron's rebellion against Moses was that they didn't like him being lifted up in the sight of all the people. They thought, *God speaks through us too, so why is Moses lifted up, and we aren't? Shouldn't we be up there too? Aren't we just as important?* Although they claimed that marrying the Cushite woman was the problem, it really wasn't what bothered them.

This is common among the rebellious. They complain to everyone about some obvious fault the leader has, but it is just a smoke screen that hides the real motivation behind their rebellion. As a leader, I have seen this happen many times in the church. People who rebel may never reveal the whole truth of what is truly bugging them, so they use an obvious flaw as their platform to speak. They'll point out the obvious human imperfection as a means to discredit a leader and promote themselves. It's too bad God doesn't feel the same way. He knows everyone has imperfections, but that doesn't necessarily disqualify them from leadership.

The Equality Problem

Does He not also speak through us? –Numbers 12:2b

The equality problem has been common throughout religion from the early days until now. It has been, and will continue to be, a strong motivation for rebellion in God's people, especially concerning leadership. It is the idea that says, "Since God also speaks to or through me, why does that person get to be the leader and I don't? Are we not both spiritual people? Doesn't God speak through me as well? I have some very good ideas too!"

We have the notion that if God speaks to us, then we are on equal or greater standing than the spiritual leadership God has placed over us. This sounds spiritual and revelatory, but it is dangerous ground. Neither God nor Moses ever suggested that everyone else was of no use or unimportant. God picked Moses, and that's it. He never intended any disrespect to anyone else in the family. Some people are like that, aren't they?

For some reason, they see this whole leadership thing as personal disrespect aimed right at them. They think things like, *How come those guys get to speak, be in the so-called limelight, and get all the attention? Doesn't God speak through us as well?* Sure He does, but that is not the point.

Look what was written in Numbers 12:2: *"And the Lord heard it."* Yikes! There is a time to talk and a time to be quiet. They got it backwards, didn't they? Miriam and Aaron spoke against Moses, and the Lord was extremely displeased to hear it. It didn't matter that God had spoken through Moses' brother and sister. It had no bearing on anything. God was not pleased that they were speaking against Moses. He is never pleased when His people speak against the authority He instituted. It wasn't right then, and it isn't right now. If we talk against spiritual authority, God hears!

> *Suddenly the Lord said to Moses, Aaron, and Miriam, "You three come out to the tent of meeting." So the three of them went out. Then the Lord descended in a pillar of cloud, stood at the entrance to the tent, and summoned Aaron and Miriam. When the two of them came forward, He said: "Listen to what I say: If there is a prophet among you from the Lord, I make Myself known to him in a vision; I speak with him in a dream. Not so with My servant Moses; he is faithful in all My household. I speak with him directly, openly, and not in riddles; he sees the form of the Lord. So why were you not afraid to speak against My servant Moses?"* —Numbers 12:4–8

I like what God said to them about Moses. He told them Moses was faithful in all God's household. I think this is a lost idea to the rebellious who only desire their own way. They fail to realize the importance God places on being faithful to the household of God. That was the difference between Moses and his siblings. Just being spiritual isn't the deciding factor in what God thinks about His servants. Notice how God sees things differently than we do. He commended Moses for being faithful to the whole household of God. While Aaron and Miriam felt on equal footing with Moses, they overlooked this matter of faithfulness to the people of God. Some believe it is just a matter of being spiritual that gets God's attention, but that is a mistake.

YES, IT IS TRUE THAT MANY CAN OPERATE IN SPIRITUAL
GIFTS AND HEAR FROM THE LORD, BUT TO TRULY CAPTURE
THE HEART OF GOD, ONE MUST BE FAITHFUL TO HIS HOUSE.

This is a common error made by those who speak out against the church or church leaders. They don't understand the idea of being faithful to the church, which is God's household. God values people who are faithful to His entire house, not just to part of it. Yes, it is true that many can operate in spiritual gifts and hear from the Lord, but to truly capture the heart of God, one must be faithful to His house. Being spiritual gives no one the right to speak against God's leaders!

In my years in church life, I have had many opportunities to disagree with leadership, and have been tempted to speak against them, but something always held me back. What was it? It was fear, plain and simple. Even now, I am still too afraid to speak out against them. Even if they are wrong, I still don't want to open my mouth. Why? To me, Moses represents current spiritual leadership, and God wasn't impressed with his siblings when they attacked him.

As a matter of fact, I don't even give much thought to speaking against any authority at all, be it spiritual or natural. Some people love to speak against authority, but I am not for it. When people begin to speak against the Prime Minister of Canada, the President of the United States, or local political authorities, I hold my peace. The Bible tells us to pray for all those who are in authority, not mock or criticize them. If I am going to speak something, it is going to be in prayer.

GOD'S RESPONSE

The Lord's anger burned against them, and He left. As the cloud moved away from the tent, Miriam's skin suddenly became diseased, as white as snow. When Aaron turned toward her, he saw that she was diseased and said to Moses, "My lord, please

*don't hold against us this sin we have so foolishly committed.
Please don't let her be like a dead baby whose flesh is half eaten
away when he comes out of his mother's womb." Then Moses cried
out to the Lord, "God, please heal her!* –NUMBERS 12:9–13

Some folks think they can say and do anything, and God doesn't care.
Are they ever mistaken! Just because we think we can say anything and
get away with it, we must not believe that for a second. It appears God
did care since He departed when they criticized Moses. Interestingly
enough, after God left, Miriam became afflicted with a skin disease. I
believe that if we speak against spiritual leadership, we run the risk of
chasing God away from us. If we seek to chase leadership away, we will
be the ones that God leaves in the dust. I don't know about you, but I
want God with me, not against me. If we speak against leadership, God
may start to speak against us. That is not a risk I'm willing to take! If it
happened to Miriam, it could certainly happen to me.

Moses, being the good guy that he was, prayed for Miriam. I like
this because it shows his true heart of faithfulness to the people of God.
Moses prayed and wanted the best for Miriam, even though she was
coming against his leadership. This is usually the difference between the
faithful and the rebellious. The faithful will continue to be for the people,
no matter what they do or say, but the rebellious don't have the same
heart. Their critical attitudes reveal that they would not stay faithful if
they, themselves, were spoken against. The heart of the faithful will always be for the good of the people, while the rebellious will be after their
own personal gain.

We need to understand that the rebellious aren't just against current leadership; often, their real motive is to become the leadership. They
are thinking along the lines of Miriam and Aaron: *God uses us too, so
why can't we be the leaders?* While they have the spiritual qualifications to
be leaders, they may lack the heart of faithfulness required to overcome
all the struggles a leader will endure. The rebellious come against the
house while the faithful seek to lift it up. In God's eyes, faithfulness to
His household is held in the highest esteem.

The Lord answered Moses, "If her father had merely spit in her face, wouldn't she remain in disgrace for seven days? Let her be confined outside the camp for seven days; after that she may be brought back in. –Numbers 12:14

Notice the Lord would not immediately heal Miriam. He said to let her remain outside the camp for seven full days, as required by law.

Is it possible that if we speak against leadership we run the risk of being shut out from the camp? What does this mean? Well, in that day, it meant being literally sent outside the camp for seven days. They were left alone without fellowship, and had nothing to do with the things of God or His people. This is not on my to-do list!

SPEAKING AGAINST LEADERSHIP WON'T
NECESSARILY HURT THE ONE SPOKEN AGAINST, BUT
IT WILL SURELY AFFECT THE ONE SPEAKING.

I know what you're thinking: *These types of things don't happen in our day.* But doesn't the Bible speak about these natural things as being examples for us spiritually? In other words, what happened to them physically may happen to us spiritually. I believe that people who speak against leadership will not be cut off by the Lord, but will cut themselves off from the strength and power of the body of Christ. They may not realize it, but they will grow weaker and weaker outside the camp. Speaking against leadership won't necessarily hurt the one spoken against, but it will surely affect the one speaking. It is quite possible that God intended to teach Miriam a lesson and not even the prayers of Moses could change that, so outside she went! God is ever the parent doing His best to instruct His children. I would imagine Miriam would think long and hard before speaking against her beloved brother again!

The Bible records, *"So Miriam was confined outside the camp for seven days, and the people did not move on until Miriam was brought back in"* (Numbers 12:15). The last and perhaps the most troublesome result of speaking against leadership is that it will hinder the forward momentum of the body of Christ. Miriam's banishment meant God was unable to take His people to the Promised Land in the allotted time.

I think people who speak against leadership feel they are doing everyone a favour, but they are wrong. Even if they are sincere about it, they are sincerely wrong, and the punishment will fit the crime. I believe the result will not be punishment as we know it, but rather a reaping of what we have sown. Here are some examples of possible outcomes for speaking against someone:

- *God becomes angry and leaves.*

- *The person is cut off, resulting in isolation, loneliness, and spiritual weakness, almost like being a spiritual leper that no one wants to associate with.*

- *The person can hinder God's plan on the earth. They, themselves are cut off and hinder the body of Christ because the entire body is needed to carry out the fullness of God's plan, with every part working to the edifying of the body.*

MISGUIDED JUSTIFICATION

The body of Christ needs to learn this lesson. God looks at the heart, not at the outside. Miriam and Aaron spoke against Moses because he had married a Cushite woman. I am not sure of the whole extent of this, but they must have felt very strongly that they were in the right. I don't believe they would have normally spoken against Moses unless they were sure the situation demanded it. Perhaps they even thought God would be pleased with them for doing so, or maybe they believed they were speaking against Moses on behalf of the Lord Himself.

I think there is a large number of well meaning people who are speaking against many things, all the way from leadership to church structure, and they genuinely believe they are in the right and are speaking for God. The deception here is this: one can think he is so right that it becomes okay to speak, especially since he is certain God is on his side.

Many mistakenly have the idea that if they are right, then God will be for them. Well, God's history tells a different story.

MANY A REBEL HAS SPOKEN OUT OF A
SELF-JUSTIFIED SENSE OF CORRECTNESS!

Many a rebel has spoken out of a self-justified sense of correctness! Don't fall for it! We must learn this lesson: the end can never justify the means. Moses' siblings were empowered to speak because of a misguided sense of self-righteousness. While seemingly in the right, they operated out of a wrong spirit and attacked Moses. They didn't know that two wrongs could never make a right!

Up until this point, the rebellion was in its infancy and should have stopped there, but it didn't. It got worse! Some people don't stop at the talking stage; they begin to gather people and initiate a full-fledged rebellion. This never ends well, as we are soon to discover. Read on if you dare!

THE LORD IS WITH US ALSO

Now Korah son of Izhar, son of Kohath, son of Levi, with Dathan and Abiram, sons of Eliab, and On son of Peleth, sons of Reuben, took 250 prominent Israelite men who were leaders of the community and representatives in the assembly, and they rebelled against Moses. –NUMBERS 16:1–2

The narrative about Korah and the other Levitical leaders is one that never ceases to amaze and sadden me. There isn't another story in the whole Bible that so vividly demonstrates God's disapproval of people who rebel against godly authority and leadership. How quickly they must have forgotten about the previous incident involving Miriam. She spoke against Moses and paid the penalty for it by being isolated from the camp for seven days. Did Korah think that if he could gather enough leaders together against Moses, that somehow it would make their rebellion less significant in God's eyes?

I once had someone ask me why it was Miriam, and not Aaron, who had to be put out of the camp. I didn't have the answer, so all I could offer was that perhaps she was the one who had instigated the idea to speak against Moses, and thus, suffered the consequences. I have no concrete evidence to support my answer as fact, so it must be left in the arena of conjecture. However, the story of Korah seems to support it to some degree, and we must always take precautions when we want to speak against leadership of any kind.

Does this mean we can never bring up concerns to leadership or speak our minds? No, of course not! The leader has the option to agree or disagree with the suggestion, comment or complaint. Sometimes, if they disagree, they are called "unapproachable," or accused of not listening. Their disagreement can be misconstrued as something it's not, but is a leader expected to give in to every idea presented? I don't think so. A wise leader will always listen to others and take what they say into consideration, but in the end, must still do what he or she believes to be the right course of action.

What I'm saying is that we can disagree with spiritual leadership, as long as it does not become a point of contention. A disagreement doesn't have to result in a person feeling they must walk away or rebel. If a person disagrees with something and bails because of it, have they not failed the true test of love? In other words, do we only love or follow someone when we agree with them totally? Does a leader have to be one hundred per cent right in order for us to follow? Do we only submit when we think they are perfectly right? I once heard a great pastor say this, "Everybody is submitted until they are asked to submit." Too bad this is often the case in the church today.

Rebellion would be easier to handle if it just stayed in one person and didn't multiply, but sadly, that is not usually the case. Remember Eve, who ate of the fruit of rebellion and then offered to share it with Adam, who also partook of it. I don't know why Adam didn't resist and say no to Eve. By taking part in her rebellion, he certainly didn't do anyone any favours.

Sin is never happy by itself; it needs to share! I think Korah believed that if he could get enough support from the other key leaders, Moses would have no choice but to listen and give in. Just because a majority of the people think it is acceptable to think or act in a certain way, that doesn't make it so. God obviously didn't see it that way, as we shall soon find out. C'mon, what was their problem anyway?

> They came together against Moses and Aaron and told them, "You have gone too far! Everyone in the entire community is holy, and the Lord is among them." –NUMBERS 16:3a

They probably said things like, "We have had enough of you! That's it! That's all we can stomach! This ends now! Everyone is holy, everyone is special, and all of us have God with us, so how dare you presume to be a leader over us?" They just didn't want to give in to a leader, or perhaps, they wanted to be the leader! Rebellion doesn't like to submit to leadership of any kind, be it natural or spiritual. The people continue, *"Why then do you exalt yourselves above the Lord's assembly?"* (Numbers 16:3b)

The truth of what was in their hearts was revealed through their words, *"You have exalted yourselves above the rest of us!"* I like that they threw this in, *"the assembly of the Lord."* This seems to be one of rebellion's favourite modus operandi. Rebellion tries to hide behind "the Lord" or "His Word," in an attempt to validate itself. They said, "This is really the Lord's assembly, not yours, so how could you be in charge?" It was almost as if they were saying, "We only listen to God and He thinks like we do! We don't need you! Are you still so dull?" God has exalted all of us to the same sphere of authority and power, haven't you figured that out yet?

Let's figure this out. Was God among all of them? Yes. Did God set them all apart as holy? Yes; but did that give them the right to rebel against Moses and Aaron? No, absolutely not!

Here is another question: Did the brothers exalt themselves into the position of leadership over the assembly of God's people? No, they didn't; yet that was the idea Korah and his rebellious gang were trying to perpetrate. Is it any different today? Rebellion still operates the same way, so it's easy to see.

THE MOST IMPORTANT THING

When Moses heard this, he fell facedown. –NUMBERS 16:4

A REAL LEADER DOESN'T RISE UP IN REBELLION;
HE LOWERS HIMSELF IN INTERCESSION.

Moses, the meekest man on earth, fell down on his face in grief, horror, and intercession for Korah and the assembly. Moses understood the seriousness of these accusations, and I think he didn't want to see the consequences come to Korah. That is what the heart of true leadership is like. Even when reviled, criticized, or hated, they still have the well being of the people in their own hearts. They long to see them blessed and not hurt in any way. A true leader has no ambitions of being exalted; he just wants to be a vehicle to bless the people of God. A real leader doesn't rise up in rebellion; he lowers himself in intercession. This is a heart test that everyone who wants to be a leader must pass. The most important quality of a leader is to have a heart for the people!

> *Then he said to Korah and all his followers, "Tomorrow morning the Lord will reveal who belongs to Him, who is set apart, and the one He will let come near Him. He will let the one He chooses come near Him. Korah, you and all your followers are to do this: take firepans, and tomorrow place fire in them and put incense on them before the Lord. Then the man the Lord chooses will be the one who is set apart. "* –NUMBERS 16:5–7a

I love Moses' response to them. When Moses told them to burn incense in the fire pans, he was giving them a chance to function in the priestly role. I don't think Moses believed for one moment that this would fly with God, but he gave them their opportunity. If God wanted them to be priests, who was he to stand in the way? It fell on God's shoulders to settle the matter. He would decide who could come near Him in priestly duty.

"It is you Levites who have gone too far!" Moses also told Korah, "Now listen, Levites! Isn't it enough for you that the God of Israel has separated you from the Israelite community to bring you near to Himself, to perform the work at the Lord's tabernacle, and to stand before the community to minister to them? He has brought you near, and all your fellow Levites who are with you, but you are seeking the priesthood as well." –Numbers 16:7b–10

Moses told them they went too far. It's great to see the leader stand up for what is right! They were already Levites in the service of God; they should have been content with that. It's amazing how rebellion rises up when someone is simply unhappy and dissatisfied with his state of being. They want to be someone or something else. Moses told them, *"You are already honoured among the people, why seek the priesthood as well?"* They needed to give their head a shake.

Isn't this same scenario played out in the church world of today? People desire to be something other than what God has called and gifted them to be. It seems people can't be satisfied to function in whatever manner God has created them to function in. As Moses was speaking to them, so God is saying to us, "You are already accepted, holy, loved, and valued in Me. You have a unique and amazing gift, and an important calling from God to the body of Christ. Why yearn for what isn't yours?"

The psalmist says, *"They were full of envy against Moses among the tents, and against Aaron, the holy one of the Lord"* (Psalm 106:16, BBE).

The real problem was envy! They were envious of Moses and Aaron's position among the people. The rebellion of Korah and his mates was recorded three times in the Word of God. I think anything mentioned three times must be of some significance, and therefore, worthy of the highest scrutiny. God wants us to take note.

I have noticed a similar pattern throughout the church. People who are really gifted and called to do one thing, desire another. It is sometimes perplexing when this occurs, because I see people so wonderfully gifted in an area, doing what I could never do, yet desiring to do what I am doing. No longer are they happy with their function, gift or calling; they want something different.

... PEOPLE CAN BE TEMPTED TO REBEL WHEN
THEY ARE DISSATISFIED WITH THEMSELVES.

A few years ago, John Bevere spoke at our church. Since he is a world class speaker and has travelled to churches around the world, I asked him what he felt was the biggest problem in the body of Christ. He told me he observed two things about church leaders. The first problem was people operating in the wrong function. The "number one guy" should be second, and the "number two guy" should be first. The other problem he saw was that people weren't satisfied with who and what they were, and they desired to be something else. For example, the teacher wants to be a prophet, or the evangelist wants to be a teacher, and so on. Of course, this kind of thing isn't limited to the five-fold ministry, but occurs in many other areas, as well. Someone who is genuinely gifted in technology, sound, or computers, suddenly wants to be a public speaker, or a person gifted in the area of helps, now wants to be in the music ministry. The list is endless, but the same thing is repeatedly revealed—people can be tempted to rebel when they are dissatisfied with themselves.

They were Already Near!

Moses also reminded them that, yes, they had already been brought near, had a great calling to function in, and were set apart. Why would they want what he had? It was as if they thought he did it on his own, and they planned to do the same. They had to realize God put him in that leadership position. If God isn't putting you in leadership, it won't end well, even if you get the position you covet! Rebellion never ends well unless it is repented of and pulled out by the roots.

REBELLION HAS THE ABILITY TO BLIND US TO THE TRUTH!

Moses explains the reality of the situation: "*Therefore, it is you and all your followers who have conspired against the Lord!*" (Numbers 16:11a). First of all, they weren't attacking Aaron or Moses; they had conspired against the Lord. Wow! If we rebel against Godly leadership, we are rebelling against God Himself! While we may sincerely, or even innocently, believe we are acting for God in this type of endeavour, the truth is we are working against Him. Just because a person is sincere, it doesn't remove the accountability factor for what they say or do. Rebellion has the ability to blind us to the truth! This is why we desperately need a revival of the Word of God in our lives. We need it to convince, convict, and help us recognize our own rebellion. God will not overlook our rebellion just because He loves us. God's love is not a cover up for sin. Grace isn't a cover up for rebellion; it is the power to overcome all rebellion!

GRACE ISN'T A COVER UP FOR REBELLION;
IT IS THE POWER TO OVERCOME ALL REBELLION!

As for Aaron, who is he that you should complain about him?
—NUMBERS 16:11b

To me, this is the simplest, yet the most profound verse in the entire Bible. I love it because it truly expresses the absurdity of people who desire to rebel against the authority figures in their lives. Who are they that you should rebel against them? Why have you made them the target of your rebellion? For that matter, is attacking anyone worth the consequence of bringing judgment upon yourself? Who is man that we should allow him to affect our spiritual lives in any manner? What do they have that wasn't given to them by God? It is pointless to come against a man, for all that he is has been granted to him by God's grace. Why do you want to be found fighting against God's plans? Paul experienced this type of conviction and correction from the Lord when he was persecuting the early church. He quickly gave up his rebellion to operate in the calling God gave him.

We all need to remember that we have been given a certain degree of grace so that we can be happy serving the Lord. You know what? Even if Moses had stepped down and relinquished his position to Korah, it would soon have been apparent that he lacked the grace to do what Moses did. The power given to Moses and Aaron to function in their calling did not extend to Korah and his group. This is the futility of the whole thing! A person can grasp at whatever he wants, but only God can give the grace to make it succeed. Learn to submit and be happy where you are called, and if He wants to give more grace to you, great, but if not, be content.

NO MORE RESPONSE

Moses sent for Dathan and Abiram, the sons of Eliab, but they said, "We will not come!" –NUMBERS 16:12

What an amazing story! There is so much wisdom in these verses! Moses sent for two men, whom I suspect were close followers and probably even good friends with him. Moses must have relied on these men before in tight situations, hence the call. But he was in for a shock when they refused to come. Have you trusted in certain people who were, at one time, close friends who had expressed their faithfulness to you, but when the time came to stand up for you, wilted away under the pressure? As a pastor, I have seen this over and over again. People who used to value your words and listen to your advice, now want nothing to do with you. When you're preaching, they are reading their own Scriptures, or gazing at their phones. When they do make eye contact with you, they look like they've lost their best friend. These people reveal their hearts by their actions. The spirit of rebellion is at work! Just like Dathan and Abiram, they will no longer come, yield, or listen!

THE TRUTH AS "I" SEE IT

Is it not enough that you brought us up from a land flowing with milk and honey to kill us in the wilderness? –NUMBERS 16:13a

---

WE NEED TO UNDERSTAND THAT
SOMETIMES REBELLION IS JUST A HEART'S CRY
FROM A PERSON STRUGGLING IN LIFE.

We need to understand that sometimes rebellion is just a heart's cry from a person struggling in life. As we read on, more clarification comes as to why they were willing to risk God's wrath by coming against Moses. They were hanging on to some of the initial rebellious words the ten spies had spoken, and they judged the validity of Moses' leadership on the basis of their own happiness: "You didn't bring us into the land of milk and honey like you promised. In fact, we think you brought us out here to kill us! We have had nothing but trouble under your leadership." It's kind of baffling that they still didn't realize that their lack of progress and success was the result of their own rebellion. I think it is much the same today.

They fully believed that what they were saying about Moses was true. There is no other explanation as to why they acted the way they did. They were there when the spies came back and were disciplined by God for unbelief. They saw the miracles, signs and wonders. They were at the mountain when the Torah was given. They heard the instructions about not touching the mountain lest they die. They knew Moses was called by God and that he spoke to Him face to face. The glory of God on Moses' face was so strong that they begged him to cover it. In spite of all this, they still chose to believe a falsehood and rebel. They believed the lie that if Moses was a true leader, none of these "bad" things would have happened.

WE AREN'T GREAT AT GRASPING THE "TRUTH" BECAUSE
WE WANT A TRUTH THAT FITS OUR OWN IDEALS!

The truth is hard to hear! I know that some will read this book and struggle with believing what it says. Sometimes we struggle with the God of the Bible when He doesn't line up with our preconceived notions about Him. We want to believe in a God made in our own image, designed around our belief system. We aren't great at grasping the "truth," because we want a truth that fits our own ideals!

In 2 Timothy 3:7, Paul says, "...always learning and never able to come to a knowledge of the truth." How can one be continuously learning yet never grasp the truth of the matter? Simply put—we don't want the real truth. We would rather believe our own truth, one that fits our personal ideals, understandings, or beliefs.

The assembly believed they had a legitimate beef with Moses and became emboldened to speak against him. Because they truly believed Moses had exalted himself to the position of leader, they felt their actions against him were justified.

TRUTH IS SUBJECTIVE TO ONE'S BELIEFS.

The actual truth and what we believe to be true are not always the same thing. Truth is subjective to one's beliefs. That's why it's so easy to believe a lie that is littered with truth. I think Korah and his gang really and truly believed they were in the right, and because of that felt empowered to speak. We need to learn that self- righteousness is never a reason to come against another person. What a person believes becomes the foundation of truth as they see it, but ultimately it is a deception. People can be poisoned by deception because it is so close to the truth that it's difficult to tell the difference. They believe a falsehood and it becomes their truth, which they will live by, whether it's wrong or right.

SPIKE

When I was a child, my father brought home a German Shepherd dog and he named him Spike. That dog would walk us to school, come and pick us up when it was over, and he fought all the dogs in the neighborhood. He was the best friend in the whole world. He was loyal, tough, loving, faithful and true, and our whole family loved him. Then, one horrible day, he was poisoned. He was in a mess, but thankfully, he survived.

A few weeks later, Spike went missing, and our worst fears were realized. He had been poisoned again, but this time didn't make it. Since he'd experienced it before, we couldn't understand how he didn't recognize the poison's distinct odour.

How does one go about poisoning a dog? Do you just throw out some poison and say, "have at her?" No, a dog would never eat straight poison; that would be too obvious. What you do is put a little poison in a large piece of meat. Dogs are carnivores, and since they love meat, they can't help themselves. I believe that a dog can still smell the poison, but because he desires the meat so much, he is willing to risk his very life to taste what he loves.

Why am I saying this? A person can be deceived into believing something simply because he really, really wants it to be true. Just as the dog craves that meat, people who become deceived want to believe the deception. They won't believe a flat-out lie, but if you mix it in with a lot of meat, they will take a bite.

> IT'S SO EASY TO BE DECEIVED WHEN WE
> MAKE UP TRUTH TO FIT OUR SET OF BELIEFS.

In Korah's case, the partial truth was "We are all holy to God;" however, the whole truth was that Moses was set apart to lead, and they were not. It's so easy to be deceived when we make up truths to fit our set of beliefs.

Think about this for a second: God loves us! Is that the truth? Absolutely, but we all know people who struggle with the idea that a God who loves us could let us go to hell forever. Their beliefs obstruct their ability to hear the truth. This is why we must be careful to live by the Word, and not by what we want to believe. What we believe may be wrong. This is why a person can always be learning but never be able to come to the knowledge of the truth. It's as if it's just beyond the grasp of their beliefs.

LEADERSHIP WARS

Furthermore, you didn't bring us to a land flowing with milk and honey or give us an inheritance of fields and vineyards.
—NUMBERS 16:14a

Korah and his cronies used the yet unfulfilled promise of God as an excuse to rebel against Moses' leadership. This is another mode of operation that rebellion uses to justify its actions toward godly leadership. It uses the current state of affairs to judge whether or not a leader is appointed by God. It is interesting that they forgot the times when God had done the miraculous through Moses to save them from the Egyptians, kept them healthy, clothed, and fed. Too often people blame others for their own lack of success.

It is the same today. In our church, we have had people who left and they've had nothing good to say about us since. They quickly forgot about all the times they were ministered to, loved, encouraged, and yes, even corrected, all for their benefit. At one time, they were all for us— "rah, rah, rah"—and after they left, they couldn't even say one nice thing.

I heard a story about a pastor who had a heart attack many years ago. There were people who immediately left his church, stating they couldn't be under a leader who suffered from an infirmity. They said if the leader could become sick, then they might, too. What a deception that is! What a horrible bit of reasoning! That is really putting man on a pedestal, isn't it?

How can one person be held responsible for the life of another? Korah and his mates were blaming Moses for their own apparent lack of success. They should have put their trust in God, not in Moses.

WE WILL NOT COME!

Will you gouge out the eyes of these men? We will not come!
                                        —NUMBERS 16:14b

This verse was difficult to grasp at first. Up to this point in the Bible, I had never read about anyone who had their eyes gouged out. Thank God for good scholarship and commentary as it helped me see what this verse probably meant. One commentary spoke of this question as an idiom meaning, "To trick," or "pull the wool over one's eyes." Korah's followers refused to participate in any test suggested by Moses, calling him a charlatan who had already hoodwinked the people into following him.

That is not too far from what happens today. People start to believe leadership has somehow tricked them into giving their lives to the church, or to a vision, or a project. They claim their leaders have led them down the proverbial garden path. They believe themselves to be enlightened and begin to tell everyone that the church is deceived, and leaders are no longer needed. They make erroneous statements like, "God isn't in the church of today," or "Leadership is an old fashioned premise that is no longer viable." Just like Korah, they walk away convinced that the church and its leadership are responsible for everything that isn't right in their lives.

THE END IS NEAR

The Lord spoke to Moses and Aaron, "Separate yourselves from this community so I may consume them instantly."
— NUMBERS 16:20–21

While this is a worst-case scenario, we can still take a lesson from it that we must nip every rebellious attitude in our own lives. I understand that most church people would never go this far, or to these extremes, to come against leadership, but even so, there are some of these prevailing attitudes at work in the church world, and their roots lie in rebellion. There are different levels of rebellion, not all this extreme, but they can affect people nonetheless. Every bit of rebellion must be expunged from our hearts, as it will surely bring trouble if left unchecked.

God was obviously not impressed with the three people groups who spoke against Moses. First, it was Miriam and Aaron, then Korah, and finally, Abiram and Dathan. All three groups walked in some form of rebellion towards Moses. They believed they were right, but God disagreed with all of them.

But Moses and Aaron fell facedown and said, "God, God of the spirits of all flesh, when one man sins, will You vent Your wrath on the whole community?" — NUMBERS 16:22

INTERCESSION FOR THE PEOPLE IS A
NECESSARY QUALITY IN A LEADER.

Don't you just love Moses? He is a great example of a leader who was faithful to God's entire house, and this is the difference between true and false leadership. Many leaders would have just told God to go ahead and consume the whole bunch. I probably would have pulled up a lawn chair, grabbed a tasty beverage, and had a wiener roast, but Moses, once again, chose to intercede for the people. Intercession for the people is a necessary quality in a leader. You know, the proof is in the pudding. A real leader will give his life in intercession for the ones he leads, while a false leader has no such inclinations.

> The Lord replied to Moses, "Tell the community: Get away from the dwellings of Korah, Dathan, and Abiram." Moses got up and went to Dathan and Abiram, and the elders of Israel followed him. He warned the community, "Get away now from the tents of these wicked men. Don't touch anything that belongs to them, or you will be swept away because of all their sins." –NUMBERS 16:23–26

It's vital for us to see that God listened to Moses. Without the pleas of the leader, they all would have been wiped out. We need to realize the importance of good leadership and its influence for the profit of the people.

Can you see how dangerous it is for us to hang around with rebellious people? We can be influenced and even come to ruin because of it. God ordered the people not to even touch anything that belonged to Dathan and Abiram, lest they also incur what was to come. God's judgment, His plan to make wrong things right, was about to take place.

KORAH'S PLAN BACKFIRES

I hope you are getting the point! If a person or a group continues to rebel, then what will be their end? I don't know, but in this case, the end was ugly.

> Just as he finished speaking all these words, the ground beneath them split open. The earth opened its mouth and swallowed them and their households, all Korah's people, and all their possessions. They went down alive into Sheol with all that belonged to them.

The earth closed over them, and they vanished from the assembly.
At their cries, all the people of Israel who were around them fled
because they thought, "The earth may swallow us too!" Fire also
came out from the Lord and consumed the 250 men who were
presenting the incense. —Numbers 16:31–35

What are the chances of this happening today? Perhaps the reason why so many believe they can rebel and get away with it is because we don't see such a drastic outcome. However, we must remember that these incidents occurred in the natural as examples for us spiritually. If a person allows a high degree of rebellion into his life, he runs the risk of spiritual consumption—a spiritual swallowing, if you will. I can only surmise what this really means, but I know God doesn't look upon rebellion favourably, nor does He turn the other cheek when it manifests.

I didn't write any of this to scare anyone, but we do need to keep these truths in mind as we go about our lives. Rebellion doesn't have a great outcome if we let it run its full course. If we rebel, we will not get away with it. As we read these words, let's allow the fear of the Lord to come upon us, and search our hearts to see if there is any wickedness of rebellion in us. There have been many times when the Lord has convicted me of a rebellious attitude or action. As of today, I have been a believer for twenty-eight years, and I can honestly say, there is still room for improvement in me.

Still Didn't Get It ✔

The next day the entire Israelite community complained about
Moses and Aaron, saying, "You have killed the Lord's people!"
—Numbers 16:41

The very next day, after this whole fiasco was over, the entire community complained again to Moses saying, *"You have killed the Lord's people!"* I am amazed that after all that happened, they still blamed Moses. So quickly they forgot that it was God who swallowed up Korah, and burned up the two hundred and fifty "wanna be" priests. They wanted to lay the blame on Moses.

People have an idea about God and they refuse to give up on it. If something starts to get swallowed up in a rebellious person's life, he will often seek to blame leadership. We want to believe God never allows such things to happen, so we seek to accuse someone else. This is what I mean when I talk about being deceived by believing only what we want to. There may be a lot of truth in it, but there is still a part that is poisonous. The outcome for this complaining community was that fourteen thousand, seven hundred of them died by a plague. Had Moses not instructed Aaron to offer incense and make atonement for their sin of rebellion, the outcome would have been even more devastating.

COMPLAINING AGAINST LEADERSHIP IS COMPLAINING AGAINST GOD!

Complaining against leadership is complaining against God! Does this mean we can never speak our minds or talk with leaders about particular issues? No, I believe that if Korah had come and spoken with Moses about the issues in a respectful manner, instead of rising up and gathering people to support himself, it is quite possible things may have turned out much differently.

Let me give you some advice. Don't rise up like Korah, but humble yourself like Moses and come down. Don't stand too tall or too strong in your own self-righteousness concerning leadership. There are no perfect leaders, just like there are also no perfect followers. Ask the Holy Spirit to search your heart to reveal any rebellion in your life, and be quick to repent and release it.

SWALLOWED UP

Woe to them! For they walked in the way of Cain and abandoned themselves for the sake of gain to Balaam's error and perished in Korah's rebellion. –JUDE 11, ESV

A careful reading of the book of Jude reveals how God looks at rebellion in His people. Jude shows us that rebellion does not have a great ending, even if the rebel is one of God's own. His warning was *"Woe to them."* Woe, woe, woe! I don't like that word at all. The only "woe" I want to hear is when I'm riding a horse and want to make it stop— "Whoa baby, whoa," not "woe, woe, woe!" This sounds pretty scary to me, so I'm motivated to learn the lesson here. How about you?

Now we know that Korah and his whole family were swallowed up by the earth because of his wicked actions against leadership. I don't believe that will happen anytime soon to people who rebel now, but it is possible they may be swallowed up by something else. Perhaps they will be weakened as they cut themselves off from those in authority, or maybe their spiritual life will be sucked out of them. I don't know, and I don't want to find out. Here's the point: the end of rebellion is never good!

SCHOOL OF HARD KNOCKS

> *It's a school of hard knocks for those who leave God's path, a dead-end street for those who hate God's rules.* –PROVERBS 15:10, MSG

Unfortunately, it is the school of hard knocks for the one who refuses to listen to sound Biblical advice in life. I too, have often been the recipient of this kind of training, but it is certainly not my preference. The highest form of learning comes by simply listening and doing; the other is by the school of hard knocks. The school of hard knocks causes the person to hopefully learn a lesson through the experiences they have. The children of Israel went through this school for forty years, and after all that time, God still referred to them as stiff-necked, stubborn, and rebellious. I wonder if we are any better than they.

For example, what's the best way for a child to learn that the electrical outlet is off limits? Is it by listening and obeying, or by trial and error? I can remember when my son, Brinn, went through this learning experience. He had been told previously to keep his hands away from the strange little device he passed by frequently as he walked along the wall. At each passing, his curiosity must have grown because one day I heard his cry of pain. I ran into the room and found him a little shaken up and scared, more so in surprise than pain, but the look on his face was priceless. The school of hard knocks was in progress—not recommended for ultimate training.

Up until I was born again, most of my learning came from the school of hard knocks. It seemed as if I had been beaten from pillar to post for most of my life. I was so glad when Jesus came in and began to challenge the hardness, stubbornness, and rebelliousness in my life, thus saving me from more schooling. As I yielded to sound advice, and the Word of God, I was able to increase my education, but without the pain usually associated with learning. While the school of hard knocks is one way to learn, or to gain experience, it must cease to be the main way we learn. It is far more prudent to hear what others have to say about a thing than to find out the hard way.

If we refuse to get rid of a stubborn attitude, we run the risk of being put into the elementary school for hard heads. God will train us up any way He can, but His best is for us to learn by listening to His Word, and to people who are wiser and more knowledgeable than ourselves.

Obey your leaders and submit to them, for they keep watch over your souls as those who will give an account, so that they can do this with joy and not with grief, for that would be unprofitable for you. –HEBREWS 13:17

I want to encourage you to take the Word of God to heart and give up any and all rebellion, no matter the size, and become meek as Moses was. God will be with you as He was with Moses: "*A wise man will hear, and will increase learning; and a man of understanding shall attain wise counsels…*" (Proverbs 1:5, KJV).

12.

THE
CURE

I believe it is to our benefit to look for and remove every single attitude of rebellion in our lives, no matter how small or insignificant it might be. Even a little has the potential to spread like yeast and cause undue harm or trouble. There are many great blessings that God wants to bestow on us, but they will only manifest as we yield our heart, mind, and will, to walk in the humility Jesus demonstrated for all to see. If we are willing and obedient, we have an opportunity to receive the good things of God into our lives. Rebellion is the original curse released on the earth, and Jesus paid the ultimate price so we can be totally free from its evil grasp.

Now that we have discussed the many different facets of rebellion, it's plain to see that we have all suffered from it, and the question begs to be answered, is there a cure? Yes, and it is two-fold in nature. First of all, we must receive the deliverance Jesus provided on the cross. Secondly, we need to diligently guard our hearts, so that rebellion cannot take root again.

Jesus took rebellion upon Himself in substitutionary form so we could be free; therefore, we must look to Him in faith to receive that freedom, which is found only in Him. Jesus, the sinless Lamb of God, took our rebellion on the tree and purchased redemption for us, so we could be free from all sin, including our rebellious nature. Thanks to our wonderful and loving Father who sent His only Son to die for us, no one has to be plagued by stubbornness or rebellion ever again.

He was wounded for our rebellious acts. He was crushed for our sins. He was punished so that we could have peace, and we received healing from his wounds. We have all strayed like sheep. Each one of us has turned to go his own way, and the LORD has laid all our sins on him. He was abused and punished, but he didn't open his mouth. He was led like a lamb to the slaughter. He was like a sheep that is silent when its wool is cut off. He didn't open his mouth. He was arrested, taken away, and judged. Who would have thought that he would be removed from the world? He was killed because of my people's rebellion.

–ISAIAH 53:5–8, GW

JESUS WAS NOT, COULD NOT, AND NEVER WILL BE THE AUTHOR OF REBELLION.

As we've been saying, Jesus was not, could not, and never will be the author of rebellion. He was the epitome of a man who lived a life without rebellion. Not even a hint of stubbornness toward authority existed in him. He was the sinless Lamb of God, who came to take away the rebellious sin nature of the world. He was the Messiah who suffered and died a horrible death on the cross so we could be free from the sin of rebellion and all its lingering effects.

Just as Jesus took sickness on His body to provide healing for us, He also bore our rebellious nature on the cross so we could live in freedom. We must remember that it pleased the Father to place the sin of mankind on Jesus so it could be eradicated once and for all. We make quite a fuss about the substitutionary work of redemption for sin, sickness, disease, and rejection, but what about rebellion? Jesus bore it to redeem us, so why do we allow rebellion to continue in our lives? If we really believe Jesus is our Redeemer, we cannot let rebellion have any part of us. Even stubbornness must be addressed in believers. All resistance to authority, selfish ambition, and unwillingness to yield must be abolished if we truly want the finished work of the cross to run its course. We must put our faith in the blood of Jesus and receive, in ourselves, the power of God to free us from rebellion and its wicked effects.

I hope you have come to the understanding that any rebellion, no matter how small or insignificant, is not part of God's heart, and therefore must be put away from us with much haste. Honest self-evaluation is necessary if we are to overcome any stubbornness and rebellion in our lives. A person can only be free if he is willing to admit there is a problem. Denial will only work to strengthen rebellion's position. It's time to search your life, look in your heart, and ask yourself some hard questions, one of which should be, "Am I rebellious?" This is not an easy question for any of us, but it must be answered if we are to move forward in the life God has for us. The cross of Jesus will have no effect on us if we are unwilling to admit we are in need of redemption.

After we admit we have some rebellion in our lives, or at the very least a stubborn self-willed attitude, and put our trust in Jesus to be released from it, we need to guard our hearts and minds and put into practice some key principles to keep us from falling into it again. Here are just a few things we can do to keep the leaven of rebellion from increasing in our lives.

LEARN HOW TO LISTEN TO OTHERS

There is a strong correlation between being stubborn and not listening. On occasion, God told His people they were stiff necked and rebellious because they refused to listen to Him. The Bible says the little foxes spoil the vine, so we need to take note of those times when we don't want to listen as that attitude may grow into a stubborn spirit.

James told us not to listen to hear, but listen to do. Blessed are those who are doers of the Word and not just hearers. True listening is more than just hearing something. Many parents have asked their child this question: "Are you listening?" They aren't asking whether they heard what was said, but rather, did they hear with the intention of obeying. Our actions will determine whether or not we've truly been listening.

I can tell you from personal experience how listening can affect one's marriage. Isn't that right, guys? One of the attributes that a woman wants to see in her man is that when she speaks, he is all there, giving her one hundred per cent of his hearing skills. She can tell when he's not listening. This reminds me of a commercial where a man is out at a restaurant with his wife. As she talks away, he nods his head enthusiastically as if he's truly interested in what she is saying. Then he jumps up and shouts, "Go man, go!" His countenance quickly fell as he realized she had discovered he was not as enthralled with her as he was with the TV.

I have a friend who recently took his wife out to dinner, and as he was talking to her, he noticed that while she was nodding in agreement, she was actually listening past him to the couple in the booth behind them. He told us it was a surreal experience because usually it is him not listening to her, not the other way around. He was saying nice things to her, telling her how awesome and beautiful she was, and she wasn't even listening. I guess you had to be there, but it's amazing how many times people talk, but we don't really listen.

Next, there's the person who speaks before he hears the whole matter. This can be particularly annoying to others, and it's something I find myself doing from time to time. I know my secretary hates it when I don't listen until the very end, or cut her off in the middle of a sentence. The truth is it requires work and energy to be a good listener, but it is definitely worth it.

I'm going on and on here, but what's the point? It's that people who won't listen cause problems in every relationship they have, both natural and spiritual. All are negatively affected when we refuse to hear each other. In Isaiah, God referred to the Israelites as a stubborn people who were hard of hearing.

So, go now and write all this down. Put it in a book So that the record will be there to instruct the coming generations, Because this is a rebel generation, a people who lie, A people unwilling to listen to anything God tells them. They tell their spiritual leaders, "Don't bother us with irrelevancies." They tell their preachers, "Don't waste our time on impracticalities. Tell us what makes us feel better. Don't bore us with obsolete religion. That stuff means nothing to us. Quit hounding us with The Holy of Israel." Therefore, The Holy of Israel says this: "Because you scorn this Message, Preferring to live by injustice and shape your lives on lies, This perverse way of life will be like a towering, badly built wall That slowly, slowly tilts and shifts, and then one day, without warning, collapses." –ISAIAH 30:8–13, MSG

GOD GAVE US TWO EARS AND ONLY ONE MOUTH;
DO YOU THINK HE WAS TRYING TO TELL US SOMETHING?

As Jesus walked the earth in the first century, He often said, *"He who has ears to hear."* Those were wise words indeed as the unwillingness to listen has been the starting point of rebellion in every generation. This must be why James spoke more about listening than he did about speaking, saying, *"Everyone must be quick to hear, slow to speak, and slow to anger"* (James 1:19). God gave us two ears and only one mouth; do you think He was trying to tell us something?

The Bible tells numerous stories of God's dealings with His people, and the theme is fairly constant throughout. Whenever Israel obeyed and walked in the commandments and statutes of the Lord, they prospered. When they refused to take heed, then life became hard for them. When they walked with God in obedience and with a heart to love and served Him fully, they brought on God's blessings, but when they stopped their ears from hearing, it resulted in judgment. It pays to listen!

> *Listen, heaven, and pay attention, earth! The Lord has spoken, "I raised my children and helped them grow, but they have rebelled against me. Oxen know their owners, and donkeys know where their masters feed them. But Israel doesn't know its owner. My people don't understand who feeds them. How horrible it will be for a nation that sins. Its people are loaded down with guilt. They are descendants of evildoers and destructive children. They have abandoned the Lord. They have despised the Holy One of Israel. They have turned their backs on him. Why do you still want to be beaten? Why do you continue to rebel? Your whole head is infected. Your whole heart is failing. From the bottom of your feet to the top of your head there is no healthy spot left on your body— only bruises, sores, and fresh wounds. They haven't been cleansed, bandaged, or soothed with oil." –ISAIAH 1:2–6, GW*

In these verses, choosing not to listen is likened to rebellion, which leads to the mind and heart to become infected and thus, prone to failure. Like it or not, someone who continually refuses to listen will eventually end up in a boatload of trouble, hurting from head to toe. Too many troubles in our lives are self-inflicted because we don't want to hear wisdom.

My son, listen and accept my words, and they will multiply the years of your life. –PROVERBS 4:10, GW

My son, listen, be wise, and keep your mind going in the right direction. –PROVERBS 23:19, GW

I have only mentioned a few verses regarding listening, but I encourage you to look up the word "listen" in a concordance, and you will quickly notice it is a hot topic where God is concerned. Learning to listen may be the best thing you can do to overcome a rebellious attitude. I think there are some who refuse to listen to other people, and no words, wisdom or knowledge will help. They don't want to hear. I hope you aren't one of them.

In my own life, I am learning to be a better listener, to take the time and effort to hear what is being said and even be willing to yield to that wisdom or knowledge. The longer I live, the more I realize how little I know. It is a choice we all need to make, and I am choosing to listen to what others have to say. That old saying, "No man is an island to himself," still rings true today!

STOP BEING STUBBORN

I will instruct you and show you the way to go, with My eye on you, I will give counsel. Do not be like a horse or mule, without understanding, that must be controlled with bit and bridle or else it will not come near you. –PSALM 32:8–9

Being stubborn isn't always about a person who holds back; it can be manifested in the one who persists in going forward when it is not prudent to do so. The writer of this psalm speaks about both as someone lacking understanding. A rebellious person is without understanding when he resists or pushes when it is not right to do so.

Horses and mules require bits and bridles to be controlled, but God wants us to yield without the need of external devices. A horse wants to run ahead, and a mule wants to hold back. Both want their own way! Don't be like either animal; instead, be a person with good understanding and yield to the one holding the reins. If we need a good yank from someone, perhaps we have become stubborn. We should be people who are easy to get along with, willing to yield, able to take advice and be corrected when necessary. When someone has a better idea, let's be quick to take him up on it and give up our own way.

Stubborn people are very resistant to what others have to say. They get their backs up at the slightest opposition to their own thinking or ideas. They tend to have to do it their way, even if it is wrong. They are right, and everyone else is out to lunch. Hence, they can be very challenging to work with, both naturally and spiritually. Jesus wasn't difficult to get along with, nor was He resistant to authority. He didn't openly argue or shout in the streets, and He spoke in the synagogues for all to hear. He was like a sheep going to slaughter and never opened His mouth to defend His position. When He was reviled, He didn't retaliate, not even once. I mean, how yielded is that? A stubborn person would have become angry, said their peace, and fought to do it their own way. Jesus was the perfect example of what stubborn isn't and the good news is He did it all for us.

STUBBORNNESS IS JUST PLAIN OLD
SELFISHNESS GONE TO SEED!

Stubbornness is a subtle form of rebellion that causes tremendous trouble in every relationship we have. How often have I been the cause of troubles with my wife, children or in other relationships? I have allowed my stubbornness to prevent me from hearing what others had to say. Stubbornness is just plain old selfishness gone to seed! Unfortunately, a stubborn person is headed for serious trouble because it is the school of hard knocks for those who refuse to change: *"Blessed are those who have a tender conscience, but the stubborn are headed for serious trouble"* (Proverbs 28:14, NLT), and, *"Whoever stubbornly refuses to accept criticism will suddenly be broken beyond repair"* (Proverbs 29:1, NLT).

PLAY BY THE RULES

Do you know that every game has its own set of rules? Those rules make the game fun. If you take the rules out, the game becomes a free-for-all and loses its excitement and fun. No one can win a game without following all the rules of play. Life is similar in nature, having rules of its own.

I think people do want to follow the rules. Take driving for instance. What would driving be like without rules? Well, just go to India and see for yourself. I have a pastor friend who was just there and he told me about some of his harrowing experiences. He had to ride on the back of a motorcycle, so he just closed his eyes and prayed. They drive like crazy there with a first come first served attitude. The guy with the largest vehicle wins and woe to the little guy! It is mayhem at best.

In Canada, where I live, it is different. Here, we try to follow the rules of driving. Anyone who detours from these rules will find himself at the mercy of a raging driver, who will attack by yelling, honking the horn or making obscene gestures. These wonderful Canadian people, who are the most polite and helpful people in the coffee shop or mall, can be genetically altered into something quite horrible when entering a motor vehicle. When they are in the mall, they are helpful, courteous and willing to yield, but put them behind the wheel of a car and all that kindness disappears. The same people who are very merciful if you bump into them in the store will try to kill you if you do it in the car. In the coffee shop, they will instantly yield to allow you into line, but try to cut in line with an automobile and demons will manifest. The truth is this—we like our rules, except when we personally don't want to obey them. Then they become obsolete or stupid!

Paul writes to Timothy: *"Also, if anyone competes as an athlete, his is not crowned unless he competes according to the rules"* (2 Timothy 2:5). In the realm of athletics, we are quick to disqualify those who fail to win by following the prescribed set of rules, yet when it comes to the things of God, many want to win by disregarding the rules. We have some-how come to believe that we are winning when we are stubborn towards authority or rebel against the establishment or current leadership. We couldn't be more wrong if we tried. God is not pro-rebellion! He hates it and requires full obedience in His children. He may put up with it for a while when we are first saved, but the older we get, the more responsible He wants us to be. We are to be the forerunners and examples of com-plete obedience to the rules He has set down for man to follow.

Paul was explaining to Timothy that to compete for the prize, one must compete according to the rules. Isn't it true—no one really wins unless they have submitted to the rules and adhered to them? It is no different in life, both naturally and spiritually speaking.

> IF WE DON'T PLAY BY GOD'S RULES,
> WE WILL NOT WIN GOD'S PRIZES!

No one can win unless they follow the rules; there are no short cuts. God wants us to win and succeed, but not at the expense of disregarding His rules. He gave us the Bible, the great rulebook, so we could see and understand the blind spots of our rebellion, repent of them, and run the race to capture the prize. If we don't play by God's rules, we will not win God's prizes! We cannot be crowned for playing the game our way; we must play according to the instructions set down by God. If we do, He will gladly give us the rewards we deserve.

ADAM AND EVE

Sadly, Adam and Eve chose not to follow the one rule God had given to them. Think about it— it was only one rule, and it was very simple for them to follow. Their burden wasn't hard or difficult to bear. The same holds true for us today. Nothing God has asked of us is too hard for us to do. Don't think that you are hard done by because someone is asking you to follow the rules. Instead, why not start asking how you can do it better. I want Him to show me my blind spots. I want Him to reveal to me what I cannot see in myself, using whatever means He desires to do so. I want to follow the rules. When I do, I feel so much better. I want to be soft and pliable before God and people and be the most yielded person on the planet. What about you? Are you easy to get along with? Do you take advice? Are you willing to yield to someone else? Do you obey the rules but secretly hate them? Are you resistant to leadership or authority figures? Could it be you need to be delivered from a rebellious attitude?

BE A FAST LEARNER

When I was about ten years old, my friends and I wanted to have a wiener roast, so we plotted to steal some wieners from the local food market. No one, other than me, was brave enough to do it, as I was always dumb enough to do what no one else would do. I'm not sure if that is a good or bad quality. I went into the store, grabbed a pack of Maple Leaf tube steaks, tucked them in my jeans and away I went. Already being a professional thief at ten, this seemed like an easy hit, but as I raced to the door, the owner grabbed me. The police were called, my mother came, and no one was very pleased with me. Even with the addition of two pairs of pants, the licking I received from my irate father was painful as ever. Here's the funny part—my mom asked me later, "Why didn't you just come home and ask for some wieners?" Duh! The thought never crossed our minds! So it was the school of hard knocks once again for me.

For some reason, even at a young age, the rebellious nature wants to arise and kick against rules and sound judgment. Until I was born again many years later, I suffered greatly in the school of hard knocks. When I was saved and began to see the light, I was relieved that I could learn simply by listening and then doing what was right. If we are willing and obedient, we will enjoy the good of the land, but if we refuse and rebel, the hard knocks are sure to come. I've found that listening and being obedient are far better ways to learn. Are you a good listener? Are you willing to yield? Are you meek in heart and willing to hear what someone else has to say or what the Lord is saying?

I must be a slow learner, because when I was fourteen, I took my brother's car for a ride one night. Everything was going just fine until I made the last turn onto our street and flashing lights came on behind me. Oh no, the police! Wouldn't you know it; just as I pulled up in front of our yard, there they were! As the nice policeman and I were standing there, discussing the situation, my brother and his friends happened to drive up. When my brother was told about the situation, he walked over and kicked me in the shins with all of his might. Of course, he had to be wearing those five inch heel rock and roll boots that were so popular in the seventies, so it definitely hurt. As I was bouncing around in great discomfort, the policeman looked back and forth between my brother and me a few times, then got in his cruiser and drove off. I guess he thought that kick was punishment enough! Did I get away with it? I didn't think so at the time. The truth is we will never get away with any rebellion in our lives. If we don't change, it will be the school of hard knocks for us. One way or another, we will learn. If I had just followed the rules, my shins would be in better shape today.

> *So then, the one who resists the authority is opposing God's command, and those who oppose it will bring judgment on themselves. For rulers are not a terror to good conduct, but to bad. Do you want to be unafraid of the authority? Do what is good, and you will have its approval.* –ROMANS 13:2–3

Every time I rebelled against common sense and authority, I instinctively knew it was wrong and had to look over my shoulder for fear of getting caught. There is a very good reason to be afraid, for we must all face the consequences of our rebellious actions. If we resist authority, no matter who or what, we will bring judgment on ourselves.

GOD WILL REWARD THE PERSON WHO WALKS
IN TOTAL SUBMISSION TO AUTHORITY.

Rebellion brings fear with it, and all fear is torment. God has not given us the spirit of fear, but of love, power and sound judgment, so why would we want to live in torment? Rebellion allows fear into our lives, and it will torment us forever. Get rid of all fear by doing what is good and right, and you will no longer need to look over your shoulder for fear of getting caught. If you do well, are willing and obedient, you will not fear consequences, but reap a reward. God will reward the person who walks in total submission to authority. Live a life that wins the approval of the authority figures in your life and this will please God.

PLUCK IT OUT

If we are to pull out the roots of rebellion in our lives, we must pluck rebellion out from the very soil of our hearts. We must look at all rebellion as we would a plague or disease. We have to take a constant, minute-by-minute stand against every type of rebellion in our lives if we are to be free from it. It must be viewed as one of the most horrible things in existence. We cannot spend another day letting it continue to grow and bear fruit in our lives. The fruit of rebellion is just too costly. The pain and suffering brought on by mankind's rebellion has gone on long enough. Even a little stubbornness is too much in our lives. We need to be brutally honest with ourselves if we are to grasp it and tear it out. If we deny its existence, we can never be free from its hold on our lives. When we refuse to give rebellion any place in our hearts, attitudes and actions, it will begin to die. We need to establish a sign in our hearts that says, "No rebellion here!" Let's pull the root of rebellion out of our hearts and watch what will grow in its place. We will be amazed at what God will do.

> *If ye be willing and obedient, ye shall eat the good of the land: But if ye refuse and rebel, ye shall be devoured with the sword: for the mouth of the Lord hath spoken it.* —ISAIAH 1:19–20, KJV

I want to encourage you to begin pulling out the roots of rebellion in your life. I have been working at this since the day I was first saved, and the more yielded to the Word of God I am, the better my life becomes. Many of the hardships I experienced over the years were just a byproduct of rebelliousness and the hard knocks were a reminder of the consequences of it. If we live by the sword, we'll die by the sword! We reap what we sow!

JESUS —OUR SUBSTITUTE

Willing and obedient are the direct opposite of rebellion. In order to reap a good harvest, we must be willing and obedient. This means we submit out of a good and willing heart, not out of fear of being caught. We do it because we want to. We have a good attitude and then we walk in obedience to the authority figures in our lives. If we do, good will come to us; it's just a matter of time. We will reap if we continue to do what is right and don't give up.

> *At the festival the governor's custom was to release to the crowd a prisoner they wanted. At that time they had a notorious prisoner called Barabbas. So when they had gathered together, Pilate said to them, "Who is it you want me to release for you—Barabbas, or Jesus who is called Messiah?" For he knew they had handed Him over because of envy. While he was sitting on the judge's bench, his wife sent word to him, "Have nothing to do with that righteous man, for today I've suffered terribly in a dream because of Him!" The chief priests and the elders, however, persuaded the crowds to ask for Barabbas and to execute Jesus. The governor asked them, "Which of the two do you want me to release for you?" "Barabbas!" they answered. Pilate asked them, "What should I do then with Jesus, who is called Messiah?" They all answered, "Crucify Him!" Then he said, "Why? What has He done wrong?" But they kept shouting, "Crucify Him!" all the more. When Pilate saw that he was getting nowhere, but that a riot was starting instead, he took some water, washed his hands in front of the crowd, and said, "I am innocent of this man's blood. See to it yourselves!" All the people answered, "His blood be on us and on our children!" Then he released Barabbas to them. But after having Jesus flogged, he handed Him over to be crucified. —MATTHEW 27:15–26*

This is the account of the fully guilty and rebellious Barabbas being set free while the truly innocent one, Jesus, was crucified in his place. Even Pilate knew Jesus was innocent of all charges of rebellion, but it had to be the innocent in exchange for the guilty, the sinless for the sinful, and the submitted for the rebellious. Jesus took upon Himself the rebellion of all mankind. We are all guilty of rebelling and are deserving of death and yet, Jesus, by His grace, took our place and let us go scotfree. I doubt Barabbas had even the foggiest notion what was taking place and whom he represented. He was set free, representing rebellious man, and given a second chance to do whatever he wanted. We have been given a new lease on life. Our rebellion has been forgiven, but do we realize it and fully grasp what it means. Will we yield our lives totally to be Christ-like or will we continue to allow rebellion to exist? If you have given your life to Jesus, then He has become your substitute and offers a new way of thinking and living, free from all forms of rebellion. Will you take it?

Paul writes, *"He made the One who did not know sin to be sin for us, so that we might become the righteousness of God in Him"* (2 Corinthians 5:21). Jesus is our example of a man who lived His life as the most yielded, submitted and non-rebellious person ever. He never rebelled against His parents, spiritual leadership or the government. He kept the Torah, the commandments and never strayed from being totally yielded to His Father. Jesus planted the seeds of perfect submission so He could reap the fruit of perfect righteousness in all who would become His disciples in the future. We, who call ourselves God's children, have the privilege of walking out that right living day by day. Thanks to Jesus, we have the power to overcome any rebellion in our lives; past, present, or future.

Let us live our lives, not in darkness, but in the light He shines into our hearts. God has shone the light of His dear Son into our hearts, and now we can live as true sons and daughters who are one hundred per cent submitted to our Heavenly Father. We never have to give in to a stubborn or rebellious attitude again. If we allow ourselves to be cleansed from all rebellion, we will change the outcome of our lives. If we refuse and rebel, we will die by the sword, but if we listen and obey, then we will eat the good of the land.

I pray you have found this book to be of some value and that you search your heart to see if there is any leaven of rebellion there. As we repent, the Holy Spirit will convict and convince us of any unrighteousness.

He will cleanse us and set us free to live as God would have us live. If you have seen yourself anywhere in this book, my intention isn't to embarrass you or cut you down, but to enlighten and help you. If you and I are honest, we can all find a little yeast of rebellion to throw out. If you have, then pray this prayer and let the Lord begin a wonderful work in you today.

Heavenly Father, I come to you in all honesty, ready to admit that I have fallen short of your grace, and I desire to be cleansed from all unrighteousness in order to follow Jesus, my perfect example. I know Jesus took every stubborn and rebellious thought, attitude and spirit so I could be free. I have seen myself, and I repent! God, I accept your Word and Your power, by faith, to set me free right now. Thank you Holy Spirit for moving at this time and I declare my freedom! Thank you Lord, all rebellion is broken, and the blessings are released. I will be quick to hear, slow to speak and easy to entreat. I give up all stubbornness, and I will not be like the horse or the mule. From this moment on, I won't need a bridle or a bit to go in the right direction. Thank you Lord. In Jesus' name, I pray. Amen.

Notes

1. *Dictionary.com*, s.v. "rebellion", accessed October 23, 2013, http://dictionary.reference.com.

2. *Webster's Online Dictionary*, s.v. "rebellion", accessed October 23, 2013, http://www.webster-dictionary.org.

3. *The Book of Eli.* Dir. Albert Hughes and Allen Hughes. Prod. Joel Silver and Denzel Washington. By Gary Whitta. Perf. Denzel Washington, Gary Oldman, and Mila Kunis. Warner Bros., 2010.

4. *WordNet Search 3.1*, s.v. "Stubbornness", accessed October 23, 2013, http://wordnetweb.princeton.edu/perl/webwn.

5. *Christian Quotes*, accessed October 22, 2013, http://christian-quotes.ochristian.com/Vance-Havner-Quotes.

6. John Burton's Facebook Profile Page. Accessed March 5, 2013. https://www.facebook.com/johnedwardburton?fref=ts

7. *BrainyQuote*, s.v. "Ralph Waldo Emerson", accessed October 22, 2013, http://www.brainyquote.com/quotes/authors/r/ralph_waldo_emerson_2.html

8. Nancy Leigh Demoss, *Brokenness, the Heart God Revives* (Chicago, IL, Moody Publishers, 2002), 91.

9. Wikipedia contributors, "Conflict of Interest," *Wikipedia, The Free Encyclopedia,* https://en.wikipedia.org/wiki/Conflict_of_interest (accessed October 23, 2013).

10. *BrainyQuote,* s.v. "Saint Augustine", accessed October 22, 2013, http//www.brainyquote.com/quotes/authors/s/saint_augustine.html

Works Cited

Demoss, Nancy Leigh. 2002. *Brokenness, the Heart God Revives.* Chicago: Moody Publishers.

Washington, Denzel. *The Book of Eli.* DVD. Directed by Albert Hughes and Allen Hughes. Burbank: Warner Bros. Pictures, 2010.

ABOUT THE AUTHOR

Brent and his wife, Barb, are senior pastors of Faith Alive Family Church in Saskatoon, SK, Canada. He boldly proclaims that anyone who calls on the name of Jesus will be rescued, recovered, and restored, just like he was over 28 years ago, when he came to know Jesus and was instantly set free from addiction to drugs and alcohol. The best way to describe Brent's preaching style is straight-forward, with a good dose of humour thrown in. As a pastor, Brent's heart yearns to see healthy churches filled with people willing to give their lives to advance the Kingdom of God, here in Canada and around the world. Brent longs to see revival sweep from shore to shore in Canada, and God is propelling him to the forefront of a revival and unity movement in the prairies. Several years ago, he initiated the Prairie Fire Conferences, gathering many churches and pastors together to present a strong voice for revival and unity in Canada.

ABOUT FAITH ALIVE

Faith Alive is the home of The Faith Alive Show, a weekly program airing across Canada on the Miracle Channel. Faith Alive Bible College is a fully accredited Bible College offering Bachelor, Master and Doctorate Degrees in Practical Theology; Faith Alive is also responsible for Prairie Christian Academy, a fully accredited K-12 ACE school.

Faith Alive has produced 3 worship CDS – Keeper, Open the Floodgates, and Coming Alive.

Faith Alive Family Church, located in Saskatoon, Canada, has a global mandate to see God Rescue, Recover, and Restore people in every area of life. Everyone deserves to experience the Presence & Power of God, and Jesus is worthy to receive all Honour and Glory! To learn more about Faith Alive, visit us at www.fafc.ca

Faith Alive Family Church
637 University Drive
Saskatoon, SK Canada S7N 0H8

www.fafc.ca ✦ info@fafc.ca

CONNECT WITH US:

facebook.com/FaithAliveFamilyChurch   www.youtube.com/wwwFAFCca

www.twitter.com/wwwFAFCca

This captivating six track EP album containing all original songs will cause you to 'Come Alive' in God's presence as you dance to the upbeat song, "This Is Amazing Grace," fall deeper in love with God in "As The Deer," and fall on your knees in reverent worship in "Who Can Stand."

Bailey's heartfelt singing, along with the beautifully engaging music arranged by C.J Drumeller of Follow Happy Productions, and Integrity Music's Dustin Smith's expertise, is a perfect combination for an exceptional worship album.

Now Available
faithaliveband.com
or call 306-652-2230 to order

Open the Floodgates – Let it Rain Down, a live worship album by Faith Alive Band, rocketed to number one in the inspirational genre of iTunes just hours after its digital release. CD reviews compare *Open the Floodgates* with Jesus Culture, Bethel, Hillsong United, and Chris Tomlin's music.

Filled with intense and passionate praise and worship, *Open the Floodgates* draws you into the presence of God and fills you with a desire to draw closer to Jesus and give Him all the honour He deserves.